Getting the Real Story

Censorship and Propaganda in South Africa

edited by
Gerald B. Sperling and James E. McKenzie

Detselig Enterprises Limited
Calgary, Alberta

Canadian Cataloguing in Publication Data

Main entry under title:

Getting the real story

Based on papers presented at a conference held at the University of Regina in 1988.
ISBN 1-55059-009-x

1. Mass media – Censorship – South Africa.
2. Mass media – Political aspects – South Africa.
I. Sperling, Gerald B.   II. McKenzie, James E.
P96.C42S64 1990   303.3'76'0968   C90-091279-0

PN
4748
$.S58$
$G48$
1990

Detselig Enterprises Limited
P.O. Box G 399
Calgary, Alberta, T3A 2G3

Printed in Canada   SAN 115-0324   ISBN 1-55059-009-X

Detselig Enterprises Ltd. appreciates the
financial assistance for its 1990 publishing program from

Alberta Foundation for the Literary Arts
External Affairs and International Trade Canada

Funding for the Conference and this transcript were provided in
part by External Affairs and International Trade Canada. The views
contained therein do not necessarily represent the views of the
Government of Canada.

Preface

"It's **cold**", said Thami Mazwai, and he would have said it even if he had lived on the Canadian prairies all his life. Thami Mazwai was, of course, one of the South African journalists attending the conference," South Africa: Getting the Real Story", which the School of Journalism and Communications, University of Regina, organized in March 1989. We had just stepped out from the Conference venue to walk to the hotel around the corner for the luncheon event. And it was, as Mazwai noted with a wide and warm grin on his face, cold (-23°C). The speaker at the luncheon was his friend and mentor from *The Sowetan*, Joe Thloloe.

I sat at the table between the two men. Unlike the ebullient Mazwai, Thloloe is a frail looking person, quiet and soft-spoken. He asked me if the conference was timed to coincide with the international day for the elimination of racial discrimination, March 21. I said "no". Moments later, in a speech that was as understated as it was impassioned, Thloloe told of the shooting massacre in a town near Johannesburg that led to the United Nations' declaration of the day, and other stories, "human stories of suffering, of pain, of courage, of love", stories that, he said, went untold because of self- rather than imposed censorship and because journalists sometimes sacrificed their "ideals for the comfort of the very easy story".

Thloloe and the other South African journalists who came to the conference represented those who had chosen *not* to follow the comfortable path to the easy story. Instead, the phrase guerrilla warfare was often used to describe the way these journalists practised their profession under South African laws. Their papers in this book are evidence of their individual and collective idealism, acumen and an almost heroic effort to reconcile their commitment to the struggle against apartheid on the one hand and the highest standards of journalism on the other. In a day and age when journalism is sometimes perceived as being not much more than the pompous, parasitic pursuit of the trivial and the transitory, these brave journalists did a lot to restore one's faith in the integrity of the profession.

It should not in any way belittle the contribution of others to say that it was the powerful personal testimonies of the South African journalists that made this conference special for us. The sentiment was reciprocated by Max du Preez in his concluding remarks: "South Africans are getting tired of flying all over the world and attending conferences . . . to make conference delegates feel better after a session of South Africa bashing . . . and then we go home as if nothing has happened. I am glad to say that this has not been a conference like that. It is valuable for me to see the level of commitment from people here and to share in the knowledge of some of the speakers here. And also to talk with my colleagues, something that we don't often do at home on these matters . . . I thank you very very much".

Thank you Max du Preez, and everyone else who participated, for making the conference meaningful. The organization of the conference was a truly collective effort and I take this opportunity to thank my colleagues in the School of Journalism and Communications for planning it: Jill Spelliscy, Nick Russell, Jim McKenzie, Gerry Sperling, Larry Todd and Lorne McClinton, as well as the School's administrative assistant, Betty St. Onge, Secretary Georgina Fluter and Ted Bowen. After the planning was done, the person who put it all together and pulled it off was conference coordinator Mari Stewart, ably assisted by Leanne Welsh and Delores Brooks. The contribution of the Department of External Affairs has been acknowledged elsewhere. However, I would like to thank the one person who was my constant link to the Department throughout the project, SuzAnne Cormie. The conference would not have been possible without a strong commitment from the University of Regina. I am particularly grateful to the Dean of the Faculty of Arts, Dan de Vlieger, for his unstinting support and encouragement. Last but not least, the co-editors of these transcripts deserve accolades for taking the time to do this during a very busy term. The editor for Detselig was Leslie Chapman. The conference proceedings were transcribed by Marty Barker and additional transcribing was done by Leanne Osborne of the Political Science Department.

This book brings back very warm memories of some very cold days. I trust that you will find the effort worth while.

Satinder (Sat) Kumar, Director
School of Journalism and Communications
University of Regina

Contents

Introduction 1

1 Putting Censorship in Perspective

Joe Thloloe 13
Heribert Adam 19
Henry Isaacs 25
Gwynne Dyer 32

2 Being a Journalist in South Africa

Phillip van Niekerk 39
Anton Harber 42
Ameen Akhalwaya 50
Max du Preez 58
Thami Mazwai 62
Harvey Tyson 68

3 Getting the Story Out

Anthony Giffard 85
Patrick Nagle 91
Nigel Wrench 95
Govin Reddy 103

4 Picture Power

Brian McKenna 111

George Hoff 114

Sharon Sopher 117

Peter Davis 123

5 Influencing the Influential

William Hachten 135

Anthony Giffard 140

Francis Meli 150

Angus Gunn 155

Resolutions 161

Statement by Michael Valpy 163

Reply by Patrick Nagle 167

Introduction

It would have been virtually impossible under the laws and regulations in effect in 1989, for South African journalists to gather in their own country to discuss openly the assault upon the media that had been a hallmark of the National Party government. This introduction will describe the social and economic context of South African censorship and propaganda and will attempt to bring events since March 1989 up to date.

As far as the censorship and propaganda is concerned, there seemed to be little difference between the approach of the Botha government and that of F.W. de Klerk who became State President in September 1989, that is, until de Klerk's bombshell speech to the South African parliament on February 2, 1990.[1] In that address, the State President legalized the African National Congress (ANC), the Pan-Africanist Congress (PAC) and the South African Communist Party. He abolished the media emergency regulations as they applied to newspapers, although the regulations still applied to the televised filming and photographing of disturbances. He also declared a moratorium on executions.[2] And then, on February 11, as promised in his speech to parliament nine days earlier, the legendary leader, Nelson Mandela was released after 27 years in prison.[3]

Before one begins a discussion of the press, it is important to touch on the enormity of general repression by the regime to note that over the past five years, *according to government figures*, 5,000 people had died in the wake of political struggle. Only two of these were white, more than 30,000 people had been jailed without charge and

---

1 "South Africa praised worldwide", *The Leader Post*, February 3, 1990, and Phillip van Neikerk, "Ban on ANC is lifted", *The Globe and Mail*, February 3, 1990.
2 "Season of violence over, de Klerk says", *The Globe and Mail*, February 3, 1990.
3 "Free at last: Today is it for Mandela", *Miami Herald*, February 11, 1990. It may be worth quoting from an early announcement by Mandela to get the measure of the man. In 1961, soon after going underground in South Africa, he issued a press release, which concluded as follows: "For my own part I have made my choice, I will not leave South Africa, nor will I surrender. Only through hardship, sacrifice, and militant action can freedom be won. The struggle is my life. I will continue fighting for freedom until the end of my days." Nelson Mandela, *The Struggle Is My Life*, Pathfinder Press, New York, 1986, p. 121.

only now are we becoming acquainted with the existence of a murky internal government conspiracy engaged in a campaign of assassination.[4]

High on the list of matters to be negotiated between the government and the ANC are those of "grand apartheid" — the denial to Africans of the right to own land outside the 13 per cent of the country "reserved" for them and the restriction of African political rights to the election of local authorities in "homelands" and segregated townships.[5]

The University of Regina conference on the media was held in late March 1989; by September of the same year, it was still not clear that the situation was improving. While police permitted protest demonstrations during that month, 100 journalists were arrested while covering those demonstrations. Both mainstream and alternative newspapers were suffering. Max du Preez is the courageous editor of *Vrye Weekblad*, which a Canadian embassy official has called "an amazing little paper". It is the only anti-apartheid publication in the Afrikaans language. At the conference he stated that he thought that the government's strategy was "to bleed us to death". In the fall of 1989, he was given a six-month jail sentence suspended for five years for quoting one of the 543 "listed" people whom the government have decreed cannot be quoted. He awaits with some trepidation the possibility of again being charged for this insane offense and this time being thrown into jail. This charge has not been stayed as of this writing.[6]

Even Times Media Limited, characterized in this volume by South African free-lancer Phillip van Neikerk as becoming "increasingly reactionary", had been fined 2,000 rands for printing the name of a banned person. All of the draconian regulations instituted by P.W. Botha in the course of the four-year state of emergency remained in effect for almost a full year after the Regina conference.

One co-editor of this volume observed first hand the problems facing journalists in South Africa during a two-month visit in the summer of 1988:

> I talked to reporters who had been locked up by the police. I met editors who worried that their newspapers would be shut down. I spoke

---

4 Pauline H. Baker, "A Start On Dismantling South Africa's Secret Government", *Manchester Guardian Weekly,* December 24, 1989, page 18.

5 George M. Frederickson, "Can South Africa Change?" *The New York Review of Books,* October 26, 1990.

6 Telephone interview with Ameen Akhalwaya, editor of *The Indicator,* March 8, 1990.

to journalists who told me they feared having their homes fire-bombed in the middle of the night by government agents posing as terrorists. A couple of black journalists told me they expected their profession would lead them to an early death.

I met others who were preoccupied with less dramatic concerns, such as whether their stories might break the laws regarding one of the hundreds of "listed" and "banned" persons who have been placed in a state of official non-personhood as far as the media are concerned. They couldn't be quoted in the paper, under penalty of imprisonment . . . [7]

Thus journalists could be barred by police from the scene of any "unrest" as defined by the police; and they could be removed by the police from such places. It was illegal to report on actions taken by the authorities to quell resistance and publications could even be "obliged to make use of the official report on such events".[8]

As Ameen Akhalwaya, editor of *The Indicator,* notes in his paper in this volume, the journalists' ingenuity was stretched to the limit in dealing with regulations, which made it "illegal under the emergency to report on consumer boycotts, school stay-aways, general strikes, if the article could be construed to be promoting the action."[9] Detention of protesters and their situation in jail could not be reported unless the police confirmed the details. "It [was] even illegal, strictly speaking, to record the release of the detainee."

Anton Harber, co-editor of *The Weekly Mail,* was still in the thick of things when we spoke to him by phone on November 7, 1989. Paradoxically, while he said then that "the new president was moving faster than the last one ever thought of moving," he was finding himself under increasing legal harassment from the government. He was facing two charges for breaking the emergency regulations and one for violation of the Internal Security Act in that he had quoted a "listed" person. All these charges were dropped on February 2, 1990, "simultaneous with de Klerk's announcement."[10]

In March, 1989, Harber had said that "you have to have the street fighter's desire to spill blood on the streets, I'm afraid, and get involved in scraps on street corners rather than in the courts." In

7 Jim McKenzie, "Getting the real story doesn't get the whole story", unpublished manuscript, December 1989, page 10
8 "South Africa: Brutal censorship continues", *Southern Africa Chronicle,* December 11, 1989, pages 1-2.
9 *Ibid.,* page 2.
10 Telephone interview with Anton Harber, March 8, 1990.

November, 1989, we asked him if he still considered himself a street fighter. His answer: "These days I'm a court fighter. Most of us editors are spending half our life in the courts."

And yet, in March of 1990, though excited about the future, Harber was apprehensive. He said there were still laws that restricted all sorts of things.

> A major one would be the Internal Security Act which still gives them the power to close newspapers, which bans us from quoting certain people even though they have taken most of the names off the list. There is the Prisons Act, the Police Act, the Defense Act.[11]

A rather different reaction, to the de Klerk liberalization moves comes from *The Indicator*'s Ameen Akhalwaya. He has grown so used to the repression that he finds its removal "weird":

> The problem is . . . suddenly we feel very uncomfortable about somebody *not* looking over your shoulder. It's such a weird feeling, because it's the first time [it's] happening in my journalistic career which goes back 18 years. You know, I'm sort of writing without really looking over my shoulder thinking, "Are we going to break the law if we say this or should we sort of rephrase . . . and sort of quote Mbeki or Tambo without quoting them?" This is a readjustment period for us as well . . . It was so deeply ingrained in us to work with this type of axe hanging over us that we are not entirely comfortable. We just suspect that somewhere in the background the Nationalists are lurking and they can make it illegal anytime they feel like it. It's just a very weird feeling.[12]

Paradoxically, the new freedom seems to be making the newsgathering process somewhat less exciting as well. Although feeling good about all the changes introduced by de Klerk, Akhalwaya commented almost nostalgically in March 1990.

> We are printing this weekend and oddly enough, we haven't got a lead story because the paper looks very thin newswise. All these developments are . . . coming . . . but there is nothing substantial from any quarter. You know, before, we always had either somebody being detained or some human rights violation. It was always readymade. Suddenly that sort of thing has eased off completely.[13]

The question arises as Canadian government attitudes towards South Africa. And this matter came up at the conference. Some representatives of Canadian Non-government Organization (NGOs)

---

11 Ibid.
12 Telephone interview with Ameen Akhalwaya, March 8, 1990.
13 Ibid.

felt that the issue of sanctions should be discussed at the conference. On the other hand, conference organizers and journalists from South Africa thought that the purpose of the gathering was primarily to discuss questions of South African media censorship and propaganda. In the end, all agreed not to debate sanctions.

And yet, the issue cannot be ignored completely, even in this context. For there are those who say that Canadian government sponsorship of this conference was a ruse by the Canadian government to detract attention away from its failure to apply full and unequivocal sanctions. Indeed, for years, NGOs and anti-apartheid activists have been highly critical of Canadian government policy, first with regard to the government's benign approach to Canadian corporations and banks with investments in South Africa, and latterly with regard to Canada's weak-kneed approach to sanctions and its reluctance to embrace the ANC because of its armed struggle policies and alliance with the South African Communist Party.[14]

According to Lucy Edwards, who until November 1989 was political affairs counsellor at the Canadian Embassy in Johannesburg, even if there were full and comprehensive sanctions, support for a free press and the struggle against South African government propaganda and censorship would still be necessary. The argument within External Affairs and with some of the NGOs and anti-apartheid groups is:

> . . . not a disagreement over principle; it is a disagreement over timing, volume and impact . . . We are arguing over tactics. The [Canadian] government has said that . . . if there is no change and nothing else seems to work, we will impose mandatory comprehensive sanctions.[15]

And the debate over sanctions will continue in spite of the de Klerk reforms. Nelson Mandela wants them continued until apartheid is fully dismantled; ("To lift sanctions now would be to run the risk of aborting the process towards the complete eradication of

---

14 For examples of Canada's trepidation regarding the ANCs armed struggle policy and some NGO reaction see "South Africa: Joe Clark meets Mandela" and "South Africa: Aid workers criticize Canada's position", both in *Southern Africa Chronicle*, March 12, 1990, pages 1-2.

15 Telephone interview with Lucy Edwards, November 14, 1989.

apartheid");[16] Joe Clark will maintain the Canadian version of sanctions for the time being, and Margaret Thatcher has lifted British sanctions.[17]

It is clear that the South African government has not been able to ignore the effects of sanctions upon the economy. A broadcast in November 1989, on the official South African Broadcast Corporation stated the de Klerk government's attitude, and certainly presaged the February 1990 concessions to the ANC:

> Sanctions can no longer be brushed aside as irrelevant or easily surmountable. The starting point is to acknowledge that sanctions have . . . serious influence on the national economy. They have as well had an adverse effect on social conditions through their influences on job creation, unemployment and standards of living. South Africa, in order to deal with them, has got to embark upon positive and dynamic social and constitutional reform.[18]

Whatever the effect of Canadian sanctions policy, it is clear that the attempts by the Canadian Department of External Affairs to make known the extent of South African government and propaganda policies and the actual material support that the Canadian embassy has funnelled to South African journalists fighting for a freer press has been substantial.

Lucy Edwards explains that Canada has been the catalyst for the creation of the "Defense Trust" which engages lawyers and other relevant specialists who identify those cases of censorship by the government that are worth taking to the courts. Money from the Trust is used to defend journalists and newspapers facing trial.

> They [the Trust] will also take cases where there is a good chance of striking down regulations and laws in order to expand freedom of

---

16 "What Nelson Mandela Said", *Manchester Guardian Weekly,* February 18, 1990, p. 18.

17 "Mulroney credits sanctions for de Klerk's 'courageous decision' "*The Globe and Mail,* February 3, 1990. Ameen Akhalwaya says that he has evidence that the de Klerk government was motivated by the prospect of European integration in 1992, with South Africa being excluded because of its apartheid policies. Akhalwaya first got wind of this theory in March of 1989, in conversations with South African exiles in Canada. He came to Canada, of course, to attend "The Real Story" conference. He says that he confirmed the story at the Commonwealth secretariat in London on the way home. He concludes that Margaret Thatcher's rush to remove sanctions was her way of fulfilling the deal with de Klerk. Telephone interview with Ameen Akhalwaya, March 8, 1990.

18 SABC Broadcast, November 6,1989, as transcribed by Ray Louw, Chairman of the Save the Press Campaign.

the press . . . It is terrific. The cases they have taken on have been quite impressive and they have won more than they have lost which in South Africa is always astonishing.[19]

In addition to being the major funder for the Defense Trust, the Canadian Embassy has been financially supporting such groups as the Anti-Censorship Action Group and the Save the Press Campaign. As Edwards says, "[We] . . . help them with their bills for information and for education of the [South African] public about why it is important to fight censorship . . ."

When the Canadian embassy embarked on its anti-censorship campaign in South Africa in fall of 1988, it recognized that one thing that South Africa was short of was qualified black journalists. According to Edwards, "There was a need identified very early on for a critical mass of talented journalists who were black, primarily but not exclusively, to come into the media in the alternative press and elsewhere."

One result of closing down the *Rand Daily Mail* in 1985, mentioned by Phillip van Neikerk in his essay in this volume, was a substantial exodus of journalists from South Africa to Canada and Australia. The news just wasn't getting out to the South African people. Another result was the rise to prominence of such alternative papers as the *Weekly Mail* and *The Indicator.*

The Canadian government found itself in something of a dilemma. It knew that it was essential that these fledgling newspapers receive financial support for day to day expenses. The embassy also recognized that these alternative papers were themselves good vehicles for training. On the other hand, the Canadian embassy was sensitive to the Infogate or Muldergate affair described in this volume by Anthony Giffard wherein the South African government bought domestic and overseas newspapers to use as propaganda vehicles.[20] In other words, the Canadian Embassy, did not want to be accused of doing the same thing as the South African government, that is, using state funds to support newspapers. In the end the Embassy realized that to compare the activities of a racist regime intent on a worldwide campaign of disinformation with Canadian financial support for the training of South African journalists and for equipment to keep the alternative press alive was nonsensical.

---

19 Telephone interview with Lucy Edwards, November 14, 1989.
20 See also George Martin Manz, "The Lie Machine", *Briarpatch,* February 1989, pages 19-24.

Indeed Canadians, through their taxes, have not only been supporting in-house training programs in such alternative newspapers as the *Weekly Mail* and *Vrye Weekblad,* they are also making financial contributions to the creation of a free press in Namibia. In 1988, the *Namibian,* (a pro-South West Africa People's Organization [SWAPO] newspaper) was blown up mysteriously. Lucy Edwards without hesitation admits.

> We announced the following day a grant of $100,000 to rebuild the *Namibian.* Quite frankly it was wonderful not to have to worry about policy . . . but just do the right thing.

However important may be questions of censorship and propaganda in the current context, an understanding of the larger political and social context is also essential. For example, while the Democratic Party in South Africa is considered to be "leftist" on the spectrum of white parliamentary parties and is certainly unstinting in its denunciations of apartheid laws, "it is unequivocal in its commitment to free market capitalism and its rejection of socialism."[21] Of course, all the hitherto illegal formations from the ANC, the United Democratic Front (UDF), the South African Communist Party, and the PAC, have "radical democratic" rather than "liberal" economic and social platforms.

"They put emphasis not on individual or minority rights or on preserving a capitalist or mixed economy but rather on turning over power to an underprivileged and dispossessed majority that will likely prefer socialism and the redistribution of wealth."[22] This commitment to the use of the state as an instrument of social policy on the part of the black opposition is made more understandable when one looks at the social and economic conditions facing non-whites in present-day South Africa.

A recent study, *Uprooting Poverty* by Francis Wilson and Mamphela Ramphele reveals some alarming figures:

> Fifty per cent of the total South African population and almost two thirds of the African population earn less than is required for subsistence. One third of all black children (including "coloreds" and Indians) are victims of malnutrition. The infant mortality rate, estimated at between 94 and 124 per thousand births during the early 1980s, is considerably higher than that of the more prosperous African countries

---

21 Raymond Bonner, "A Reporter at Large—Choices", *The New Yorker*, December 25, 1989.
22 Frederickson, page 51.

such as Kenya and Zimbabwe and roughly equal to some of the poorest . . . The best available estimates put the jobless rates at around 20 per cent for the labour force as a whole and up to 50 per cent or even higher in districts where blacks are concentrated.[23]

South Africa both exports food and supports a very high standard of living for its white population. "It has in fact the most unequal distribution of wealth and income of any country in the world."[24]

While there were some economic gains for some blacks during the 1970s, in general there has been increasing black unemployment and further deterioration of rural resources in areas where most blacks live. Millions of blacks have been forced to move from one place to another by virtue of the apartheid laws, engage in migratory labor (many travelling up to six hours a day going to and from their jobs). The results have been extreme poverty and its concomitants; demoralization, crime, disease and the aforementioned high mortality rates . . . and all of this as a result of conscious policy on the part of the South African government. (The South African government seems belatedly to have begun to recognize not simply the inequities of apartheid, but the economic idiocy of such policies. In the first budget brought down since the February "bombshells", the government announced the creation of a $900 million superfund "to overcome historic disadvantages suffered by blacks under apartheid". Whether this is "too little too late" will be determined by the black population.)[25]

Of course, there are two aspects to this recital of social statistics. For one thing, reporters, foreign and domestic, must continue the fight to report at home and abroad the reality of life in South Africa. The previous South African government mythology of a prosperous peaceful multiracial society moving towards some kind of rich stability along separate roads has always been balderdash. This fairy tale can be countered by reporters telling the "Real Story", that is, the story as they see it.

For the future and looking beyond the end of apartheid, it is essential that the debate over censorship be pursued vigorously and relentlessly. As noted above, it is not likely that a liberated South Africa will have a capitalist economy. As Joe Slovo, head of the South African Communist Party, and one of the few white senior members

---

23 As cited in Frederickson, page 53
24 Ibid., page 53.
25 Phillip van Neikerk, "Pretoria cuts military spending, sets up superfund to aid blacks", *The Globe and Mail*, March 15, 1990.

of the ANC executive put it, "There is no way in which you can expect the average black to accept that liberation has happened if virtually all the wealth remains in the hands of the whites."[26]

Not that capitalism necessitates a free press.[27] However, as the history of Eastern Europe over the past 40 years has shown all too clearly, those who claim to be "socialists" have found it easy in the name of their doctrine to deprive their populations of fundamental human liberties including a free press. Joe Slovo, himself, acknowledges the failures of East European socialism:

> Those who ran the existing socialist states perverted its objectives. In one sentence, its most terrible failure was the separation between socialism and democracy, which infected every level of society.[28]

Those South Africans participating in the "Real Story" conference, whatever their differing political ideologies, are attached passionately to the notion that the media must expose and oppose in the search for the truth. A liberated South Africa, as much as a South Africa in chains will need ". . . a cantankerous press, an obstinate press, a ubiquitous press."[29] The struggle for free expression and for the right to know will continue when South Africa is free. Surely, a non-racist egalitarian society cannot call itself democratic without a critical media.

Gerald B. Sperling and James E. McKenzie
March, 1990

---

26 "Mandela, exiled ANC leaders plan for talks with South Africa", *The Globe and Mail*, March 2, 1990

27 For an exhaustive study of the weak functioning of the media, or rather its role in strengthening domestic privilege in the United States, see Noam Chomsky, *Necessary Illusions Thought Control in Democratic Societies*, CBC Enterprises, Montreal, 1989.

28 Phillip van Neikerk, "South African Communists reconsider objectives", *The Globe and Mail*, January 27, 1990.

29 As quoted from Judge Murray Gurfein's decision rejecting the U.S. government's efforts to bar publication of the *Pentagon Papers* in Chomsky, page 2.

1

Putting Censorship in Perspective

Four experts review recent political and social changes in South Africa, analyze trends, and predict what the future could bring.

Joe Thloloe,
Deputy-Editor of *The Sowetan*

Heribert Adam,
Professor of Sociology and Anthropology,
Simon Fraser University

Henry Issacs,
Editor of *Frontline Southern Africa* magazine

Gwynne Dyer,
Syndicated Columnist and Historian

March: a month dripping in the blood of South Africa

"The real story of apartheid is a story of violence, of keeping blacks at the bottom of the pile."

By Joe Thloloe

I think it is very fitting that this conference takes place in March. In the South African calendar, March is a very bloody, dripping month. On March 21, 1960, the South African police shot down 69 people in a small township south of Johannesburg called Sharpeville. Men, women and children were shot. Hundreds went to the hospital, injured by bullets. And it was in commemoration of that day that the United Nations decided that March 21 every year will be the International Day of the Elimination of Racial Discrimination.

But if we thought enough blood had been shed on March 21, 1960, we hadn't reckoned with our rulers. On March 21, 1985, 25 years later exactly, in almost identical circumstances, the South African police shot and killed 21 people, and again injured squads of others in a township called Langa in the Eastern Cape. In 1960, I was a very angry 17-year-old school boy. I walked the streets of the black townships of Johannesburg when the African National Congress (ANC) organized an anti-pass campaign. The people were angry. They'd had enough of the humiliation of the pass laws; the young policemen demanding passes from them. These were documents that carried virtually their entire life histories. And they indicated if you had permission to be in "white" South Africa.

The police would raid our townships in organized fashion and demand passes from all men. Or they would do it at random. You would go out of your house and see a policeman and he would ask

Joe Thloloe is deputy editor of the *Sowetan*, South Africa's largest black daily paper. He began his journalism career in 1961 on the *World*, a paper banned by the government in 1977. He also worked on *Drum* and *The Rand Daily Mail*. Thloloe was president of the Union of Black Journalists from 1975 until it was banned in 1977. He won the Louis Lyons Award for conscience and integrity in journalism presented by the Nieman Fellows of 1981-82. Thloloe has been jailed, detained and banned. In 1988-89 he was a Nieman Fellow at Harvard University.

you for your pass. And if you didn't have it on you, they would throw you into jail. The message from the African National Congress that organized this anti-pass campaign was very simple. Leave your pass at home, go to the police station nearest to you and demand that they arrest you because you are not carrying your pass, and you are not prepared to carry it again. It was supposed to be a peaceful march, a peaceful protest.

Thousands went to the police stations. But at Sharpeville, the police panicked and opened fire. We were already in the police cells in Orlando when we first heard the story of the massacre. Then the events started piling very fast. A state of emergency, the first in the history of the country, was declared. Hundreds of people were detained under that state of emergency. The pass laws were suspended and the Pan-Africanist Congress and the African National Congress were outlawed.

In 1985, I was a news executive on *The Sowetan* when the story of the massacre in Langa came over the wires. If any novelist had written that plot, men would have definitely dismissed it as a hopeless story. It hinged on so much coincidence, it couldn't be true. The residents of Langa were walking to a funeral in another township when they were confronted by the police. The excuses given by the police in 1985 were the very same excuses given by the police in 1960. "The officers shot in self defence at a mob that was attacking them."

So it is fitting that we meet here this week, journalists, citizens of this world concerned about South Africa and apartheid. Before we can adequately grapple with the story of apartheid, we need to accept that racism is a worldwide phenomenon. The only reason we single out South Africa is that, in that country, the racism is stark naked, unadorned. Looking at racism in South Africa will help us uncover it wherever it shows itself in this world.

In South Africa, racism was given a formal name when the present government took over in 1948. It's called apartheid. It's an Afrikaans word that means apartness. It is a name that the National Party government gave to their codification of what was practised all along. So many people want to say that apartheid started in 1948 when the National Party took over. I refuse to believe that. The National Party government merely codified what had been practised.

There are various ways of looking at apartheid. Some see it as a vertical line that separates black South Africans from white South Africans — separate beaches, separate hotels, separate toilets —

that type of thing. Those who hold this view believe that if the vertical barriers are brought down, apartheid will be dead. . . . Pik Botha, Minister of Foreign Affairs in South Africa, told the United Nations some years ago that apartheid is dead. It's in the same vein that Afrikaners are saying today that apartheid is a sin. These are the people who see apartheid as a vertical line, so if people mix together in social clubs, then apartheid has been destroyed.

Many of us have another view of apartheid. We see it as a horizontal stratification of society in terms of South African racial laws. It's a hierarchy of political and economic power and privilege. The top layer, the cream of society, are the five million whites, people of European descent. There are 900,000 people classified as Indian. They are second in this stratification. And the people classified as colored, three million of them, are third, and then the 26 million indigenous Africans are at the bottom of the pile.

We can take any set of statistics that measure power and privilege, and they'll confirm this hierarchy in South Africa. I'll take two sets of figures just to illustrate. The average monthly income of whites in our country is 1,738 rand. That of Indians is 912 rand, colored 634 rand, and at the bottom of the pile are the indigenous Africans earning 500 rand a month. You can also look at the per capita expenditure on education. The South African government spends 2,508 rand on a white child, 1,904 rand on an Indian child, 1,021 rand on a colored child, and 477 rand on a child of an indigenous African.

One thing that should be obvious is that white South Africa will do everything to maintain this state. They'll use the police, the army, the prisons, the laws, and the media to maintain that privilege and power. The real story of apartheid is a story of violence, of keeping blacks at the bottom of the pile, and the violence of keeping them under control when they are revolting against the original violence. But besides the story of the violence, there is also the story of their resistance to apartheid.

You can draw a graph depicting the history of South Africa this century. One axis would show dates, and the other axis, the level of black resistance to white minority rule. The graph would show a series of plateaus divided by sharp ridges. Each plateau and each ridge would be higher than the one before. The lengths of the plateaus would be progressively shorter, while the ridges would be broader.

We had a ridge in 1976 to 1977, and that was followed by a plateau. We had another ridge in 1984 to 1986. We've dropped down to a plateau again. But this present plateau is higher than the one before. In the ridge between 1976 and 1977, about 700 people were killed. In the ridge between 1984 and 1986, more than 2,000 were killed, and more than 10,000 were detained by the security forces. The plateau between 1977 and 1984 lasted seven years. The one before that, between 1964 and 1976, lasted 12 years.

Now on this graph you can also draw another graph that indicates spontaneous violent resistance to apartheid. It has a steadily rising line that would show organized armed struggle against apartheid. In September 1987, the Minister of Law and Order — they've got beautiful titles — published statistics of guerrilla attacks in South Africa. It is said that between 1977 and 1984, a period of eight years, 83 people were killed in guerrilla attacks. And between 1984 and 1987, which was only four years, 134 people had been killed.

The government also announced, at the end of 1987, that 28 members of the Pan-Africanist Congress and 111 of the African National Congress had been killed by the security forces. Now I have presented dry figures. But behind these ugly figures are human stories of suffering, of pain, of courage, of love.

When we first decided we wanted to be journalists, you here in Regina, and poor me in the dusty streets of Orlando — this is Orlando, Johannesburg, by the way, not Orlando, Florida — we had dreams of writing stories like this, human stories. But what's happened to our vision?

I'll tell you a very small incident. Last November, 1988, the present class of Nieman Fellows at Harvard were getting very worked up, getting ready for a press conference on December 12th to protest against the continued detention of Zwelakhe Sisulu, editor of *The New Nation*, and a Nieman Fellow in 1985. On the 12th of December, he would have completed exactly two years behind bars. Ten days before the press conference, the South African government released him from jail. But he was restricted. He was placed under partial house arrest. He could not leave his home from 6 p.m. to 6 a.m. He had to go into his house Friday night and not leave it until Monday morning. He had to report to the police twice a day.

He could not work as a journalist, and anything he said or wrote could not be published. The man was out of physical jail, but he was still in chains. When he was released, the press conference was cancelled. I argued that we had to go ahead with the conference, not only because of the restrictions on Sisulu, but because there were two other journalists still in detention. But the people who would organize the press conference told me that because Sisulu was out of jail, there would be no media interest in that particular conference. And I was told that the other two journalists are not known in the United States.

Now who defines the story here? What is the definition of the story we want to tell? I have seen foreign correspondents come to South Africa — almost all of them with the same shopping lists. They already know the names of the people they must interview — Archbishop Desmond Tutu . . . the Reverend Allan Boesak, and the rather unlikely Winnie Mandela. And of course they know they've got to interview the white politicians. They already have a list of the organizations they have to talk to — the United Democratic Front, and the white political parties.

Anything that is not in this groove is not a story. And so the story of apartheid remains largely untold. Journalists have sacrificed their ideals for the comfort of the very easy story. It then becomes even easier to blame the censorship in South Africa and to blame the fear of being expelled from that country. If I were a correspondent sent to South Africa, I would start by going to the two liberation movements, the African National Congress and the Pan-Africanist Congress, and I'd ask them for a shopping list. And I wouldn't go to just the one and forget the other.

I would supplement this list by talking to the thousands of South Africans who are in exile. But I would not be satisfied with just this shopping list. I'd move off the beaten path to go to the real story. I've seen some good stuff, emotionally moving stuff that's been done by journalists who had this imagination.

Now what about the South African media? Very sadly, some newspapers have succumbed and are already censoring themselves without testing the limits as hard as they can. And some of them have paid the price. The latest publications to be suspended under the emergency regulations are *Crossroads* and *New Era*. Both are community newspapers and they are now suspended until May 1989.

But the anatomy of the South African government's censorship is that they are blaming their own people for the massive support that the liberation movements, The African National Congress and the Pan-Africanist Congress, are now enjoying. People are now open in their support for these organizations. You go to a meeting and you see people showing their thumbs up sign for the African National Congress. You go to another meeting, you find them using the open palm salute of the Pan-Africanist Congress. You go to a funeral and you find youngsters dancing the toitoi and singing songs about the Pan-Africanist Congress. And in spite of the police and army road blocks all over the country, the liberation movements are getting arms and trained guerrillas into the country.

The government tries to read between the lines of every news story to find the reason for this change. And the innocent media are blamed for it. If you look at all the warnings and suspensions that the government has issued under the emergency regulations, you will find one refrain. The publications are accused of enhancing the image or the symbols of the two liberation movements, the African National Congress and the Pan-Africanist Congress.

Now it's very ironic, because under the *Internal Security Act*, it is a serious offence to further the aims of a banned organization. And the newspapers are not doing it. They will not risk 10 years or 20,000-rand fines. But the government refuses to accept that the media are innocent. They refuse to accept the fact that the oppressed are developing their own communication channels and their own languages.

There is a second reason for the government's behavior. It wants to induce self-censorship. In the end, we should acknowledge it is the rulers who control the media. All that the committed journalist can do is to go as far he can. And if the space gets smaller, some of us might have to get out completely.

The black journalists in South Africa have already defined their role. Officials of the Media Workers Association of South Africa have said that a black journalist is like a guerrilla in enemy territory. I know this phrase raised a lot of anger in South Africa when it was first used. But before I end, let me complete the story of the pass laws. In 1986 they were finally taken off the statute books. They collapsed because they had become too notorious, and too expensive to enforce because of black defiance of them.

Today, as we think of South Africa, let us also think of those who were killed by the oppression.

The revolution has been stalled, but this may provide an opportunity for peaceful change.

"The euphoria about the seizure of power has given way to a more realistic assessment of the power equation, and the result of this is perhaps that the South African state can be eroded but not overthrown in the foreseeable future."

By Heribert Adam

South Africa represents one of the great moral challenges of our time, probably comparable to slavery or fascism previously. To express moral outrage on these issues is an appropriate reaction. But I hope we can go beyond expressing moral outrage. We can try to do more than give a running commentary on fast-changing events. We can try to be analytical and as realistic as possible, without forgetting the principles we are trying to implement.

Frederick van Zyl Slabbert recently said, "The government in South Africa is poor in vision but rich in strategy." The opposition, unfortunately, is very rich in vision but poor in strategy. Perhaps we can try to be strategic in our thinking and focus on how to overcome that system and break the impasse, instead of merely deploring it.

I'm trying to make a clear distinction between what ought to happen, what we all want to see, and what is likely to happen in South Africa. I would argue that the often predicted revolution in South Africa has again been stalled. With the anti-apartheid forces in retreat during heightened repression, the euphoria about the seizure of power has given way to a more realistic assessment of the power

Heribert Adam is a professor in the department of sociology and anthropology at Simon Fraser University. His research has focused on ethnic conflicts, nationalism, and human rights in divided societies, particularly Southern Africa and the Middle East. Adam has published several books on South Africa, including his latest: *South Africa Without Apartheid — Dismantling Racial Domination.* He is currently working on a study of race relations and immigration policies.

equation, and the result of this is perhaps that the South African state can be eroded but not overthrown in the foreseeable future.

Activists like Zwelakhe Sisulu, editor of *New Nation*, have long recognized this. Sisulu has argued that instead of focusing on the impossible transfer of power, one should focus on a possible shifting of power. I would argue that continuing empowerment of the opposition and steady disempowerment of the government is a realistic strategy.

Contrary to media reports, the white electorate has slowly moved to the left on apartheid, but to the right on security issues. With the old apartheid certainties falling by the wayside, security anxieties have heightened. The National Party fully exploited these sentiments in recent elections under emergency regulations. Nevertheless, if I had to name the most significant trend in white politics in recent years, I would point to the increased defection of Afrikaner professionals from the National Party orbit. Several meetings between Afrikaner dissidents and the ANC have been held — in Dakar in July '87, in Leverkusen with Soviet academics, 1988 and in Harare, February, 1988, organized by Slabbert's Institute for a Democratic Alternative.

Prominent Afrikaner establishment figures have dissociated themselves in increasing numbers from their former political home. At Stellenbosch, the Harvard of Afrikanerdom, it is hard to find one reputable academic supporting the ruling group now, at least in the social sciences.

The National Party has clearly lost its ideological hegemony. There is confusion, there is a vacuum, and there is the emergence for the first time of Afrikaner opposition media. While most Afrikaner dissidents have not formally joined opposition organizations, they are sympathetic to the broad aims of the democratic movement, particularly open-ended negotiations with the opposition, with the ANC and other liberation movements, and the legalization of the banned non-racial movements.

In this respect, the strategy of the ANC, of peeling away layers of support for the status quo, has been highly successful. It does not force wavering whites to choose sides or push them over the fence. The strategy merely aims at neutralizing former government supporters. And obviously, this makes it easier to create new reference groups for those who doubt, or feel the costs of apartheid. These trends have crystalized in the formation of a new political party, the Democratic Party, in which the three existing parties to the left of the National Party have recently merged.

It consists of the liberals, English Conservatives, concerned capitalists, both English and Afrikaner capitalists, and above all Afrikaner intellectuals and opinion makers. This opposition, this white, liberal opposition, is roughly supported by 20 per cent of the white electorate at present, as opposed to 45 per cent who support the ruling National Party among whites and about 35 per cent who support the ultra-right, the Conservative Party.

It is a soft constituency on which the white democrats rely — unified by little more than sentiments against old-style apartheid seen as bad for business and the future stability of the country. The editorialist of *The Cape Times* has described the intellectual wellsprings and political motivations of these Afrikaner dissidents as uncomfortable with English institutions and traditional liberalism:

> If nothing else, they are recognizing the pointlessness of trying to organize an English minority to overthrow an Afrikaner majority. Their proper field of endeavor is Afrikanerdom itself. Nor are they liberals in the Anglo-Saxon mould but, at best, social-democrats in the German mould, with an added touch of agrarian suspicion and hostility towards English capital.

A minimal common ideological denominator characterizes the ruling National Party. It is no longer held together by shared principles or by a blueprint of a vision of the future. The binding cement of the ruling group lies in its patronage and the spoils of office. It is therefore vulnerable to splits and defections. It is utterly corrupt in other words. It is opportunistic.

You only have to look at all the scandals that are reported almost weekly. But I think herein lies the long-term chance for the democratic forces. And the surprisingly high vote for the other candidates in the succession race for P.W. Botha's job clearly shows a divided house. If some technocrats of this group were to break away and join the opposition in a post-Botha era, it would mean the demise of the National Party, which has ruled South Africa for 40 years, and then we would have a totally new scenario in South Africa.

A vastly strengthened ultra-conservative bloc would then face perhaps an even stronger anti-apartheid group and perhaps even a temporary alliance between the ruling nationalists and liberal democrats can be envisaged in the post-Botha era, once apartheid proves too costly for multinationals and the growing Afrikaner bourgeoisie alike. Now this force in power would certainly enter negotiations about majority rule. Its problem would be to make a controversial compromise stick with the ultra right. In the absence of a South African de Gaulle, a democratic government would totter at the brink of civil war with the die-hard racists on the one side, very much like when the Afrikaner fascists battled the decision of the Smuts government to enter World War II on the side of the Allies.

I think it's a pity that so far the democratic movement has ignored, belittled or minimized the threat from the ultra-right. I think it is time to consider realistic options for neutralizing this bloc, which would otherwise force a nonracial government to become as authoritarian as its predecessor in suppressing its right-wing opposition. Since the National Party is paralyzed by the threat from the ultra-right, a case can be made that the ascent of the right to political power would actually facilitate fundamental change.

Such an assumption would not have to be based on the false theory that worse is better or that reform is the enemy of revolution. A Conservative Party in power, one could argue, would be confronted with the same economic imperatives, the demographic changes and objective conditions that it promises to arrest in vain. Therefore objective trends outside government control eventually would even force a right-wing government to recognize reality just as the wavering National Party was pushed into half-hearted reform.

And it may be argued that the ultra-right in power would have two decisive advantages for a negotiated settlement if that route rather than civil war and economic deterioration is to be pursued.

First, a Conservative Party in power can legitimize a settlement better than a liberal or centre party that is perceived as soft on white interests. The right wing would make a controversial compromise stick without eliciting insurmountable opposition. Only a trusted conservative can neutralize a potentially dangerous backlash from an indoctrinated armed segment that a centre-liberal party would have great difficulty controlling.

Second, one could argue that the rise of the Conservative Party to political power would further increase the alienation of South Africa's Western allies to a point where decisive action could hardly be postponed any longer. By giving the lie to sham reform, the outside pressure on Pretoria would double. This in turn would spurn the remaining business inside South Africa into using its influence with government in a much more structured and forceful way, since its survival is directly threatened by such polarization by a pure racial garrison state.

Now, the crucial question concerns the costs of open white supremacy to the majority population. I would argue it is a facile suggestion by those who do not bear the brunt, and it does not matter much whether the National Party or the Conservative Party government sets the agenda of black repression. Those on the left who advocate polarization as a way to speed up change tend to understate the price to be paid and to over-estimate the stimuli for resistance which a totally ruthless despotism can stifle for a long time.

In this South African impasse, to my mind, the most astonishing actor remains South African big business. Big business in South Africa basically comprises four companies: Anglo-American, Sanlam, South African Mutual and Rembrandt. One would expect these boards to lobby hard for early negotiations between Pretoria and the ANC. In the absence of such negotiations, businessmen could join the informal contact groups and prepare the ground for negotiation politics.

However, after a reluctant trip to Lusaka in 1985, word went out from leading participants that support or even further contact with the ANC should be avoided. Capitalists distrust the communist influence in the ANC, although the Slovos are the more conservative and pragmatic forces in the heterogeneous alliance. It is they, the communists, who have prevented escalating terrorism in South Africa. The Communist Party, the AFCP, proposes a two-stage strategy in which socialism, I would argue, is put on ice in favor of an all-class alliance, with capitalists included, to secure the overthrow of apartheid and insure growth in a mixed, social-democratic economy, at least in the first stage.

Without the early identification of a few communist and liberal internationalists with the ANC, with the black cause, the main opposition to minority rule would not now be as nonracial and accommodating. Instead, a much more exclusive Africanist nationalist tendency as espoused by the PAC would dominate. Instead of grasping these unique opportunities, South Africa big business on the whole has quietly reconciled itself with a tenuous status quo. Its profits are still huge, particularly after the windfall acquisition of absconding foreign companies at bargain prices.

The interest to bend trade restrictions and other sanctions has driven many companies into closer co-operation with the government. The few outspoken and high-profile liberal businessmen, like Gordon Waddell, Tony Bloom or Chris Ball, have emigrated with various rationalizations covering their failure to contribute to a political solution, or even educate their conservative in-house constituencies. In the meantime, South African business continues with the ritual condemnation of apartheid.

Harry Oppenheimer even says that South Africa stinks in the nostrils of decent world opinion. That's a statement he made in March 1989. Nevertheless, the quiet profits from the cesspool continue to flow and can also be laundered. Ultimately, money is color-blind, does not smell and does not betray its origin.

The terrible predicament is that a declining South African economy would make matters worse for those who want to redistribute the unequal wealth. Moreover, the unemployed do not make the revolution. Starving and insecure people do not take political risks. They escape into religions, dreams, or alcoholism. Weaker unions would strengthen the state and capital.

Yet it is no wonder that impatient outsiders nevertheless want to raise the pain threshold. Unfortunately it is only when the costs of apartheid outweigh the benefits that the powerholders will finally enter serious negotiations.

Government uses the carrot and stick approach to hold power over blacks.

"Those standard rights which most Canadians take for granted — freedom of speech, equal treatment under law, travel, assembly, trial and due process of law — are legally denied to the black majority."

By Henry Isaacs

The salient features of South African society are well-known. The majority of the country's citizens are ruthlessly dominated, economically and politically, by a minority. Racism has been institutionalized through the system of apartheid. Those standard rights which most Canadians take for granted — freedom of speech, equal treatment under law, travel, assembly, trial and due process of law — are legally denied to the black majority.

Glen Moss, in his study of political trials in South Africa in the period of 1976 to 1979, concluded that conflict pervades South African society as the ruling class attempts to maintain its distinctive society, and only a thorough restructuring of all aspects of that society can remove the root causes of a conflict, which has taken on the proportions of a low-intensity civil war. That study was completed before the recent upsurge in mass resistance to apartheid. But the validity of the conclusions can be seen in the fact that in the period between September 1984 and December 1988, more than 4,000 persons were killed in political violence in South Africa. These statistics were compiled by the Indicator Project of South Africa at the University of Natal in Durban. The statistics expose the fact that most of the fatalities occurred after the state of emergency was declared in June 1986.

Henry Isaacs was born and raised in South Africa. He fled the country after being banned by the government in 1973. He is now executive director of African Research and Communications, Inc. in Washington, D.C., and editor of *Frontline Southern Africa*. He has been a research associate at the University of California at Santa Cruz and a visiting fellow at Yale. He works with alternative media in South Africa, writing articles on censorship and government propaganda.

The state of emergency, mass detentions of community leaders and activists, assassinations, bannings of more than 30 organizations, severe restrictions on the activities of the labor movement and other draconian measures by the state have failed to reduce the overall levels of conflict. Moss, in his definition of the structural nature of the conflict, wrote:

> In the wake of the rebellion sparked off by the black youth of Soweto in June 1976, the level and intensity of conflict forming the basis of South African society has grown enormously. The nature of that conflict, and its very quantitative size, suggests that it is structural in type. By this I mean that it is not a temporary aberration of something incidental to the fabric of society. Rather, conflict forms a very part of the structure of society in South Africa. As the ruling class attempts to maintain and reproduce that society, so the conflict itself is maintained and reproduced.

In other words, only a thorough restructuring of all aspects of South African society, and that includes the economy, the ruling political structures and practices, ideology and culture, can remove the root causes of the conflict. But rather than address the causes of the conflict, the ruling class has devised ways and means of creating the illusion of change, while retaining economic and political power. Desegregation of parks and beaches, the creation of a tricameral parliament that excludes the African majority, repeal of laws forbidding interracial sexual intercourse and marriage, and various other measures that are normally cited as the South African regime's reforms are integral to this program.

It is little wonder that these reforms have been accompanied by mass mobilization and resistance not witnessed in South Africa since the '50s. In 1976, the Soweto uprising marked the beginning of a decade of black protest that steadily sapped and hemorrhaged the white power structure from below. During this period, the independent labor movement that emerged after the strikes by black workers in 1972 and 1973 grew in strength and organization, gaining increasing recognition by capital and ultimately in 1979, legal recognition by the state. Perennial student boycotts in protest against the inferior system of education resulted in the almost permanent closure of many schools and as the economy went into recession, community resistance to increased rents and transportation. Costs not only increased, but we also saw the emergence of grassroots and community organizations to address local issues.

Military actions by the national liberation movements, principally the African National Congress, increased in frequency and sophistication. The former security police chief, Brigadier Zietsman, in an interview with a government-funded magazine *To The Point*, paid the national liberation movement a back-handed compliment when in acknowledging clashes between ANC freedom fighters and security forces in rural areas in the Eastern Transvaal near the Mozambican border, he said:

> People must not think this is a recent phenomenon with simple solutions. It has been going on for a long time and is more complicated than people realize. We are now picking the fruits of years of work by those who fled the country in the '60s.

He added that the intensification of guerrilla activity was partly the results of change of status of South Africa's neighboring states. Freedom fighters received training and support closer to home. However, they tried not to engage South African forces for fear of embarrassing their hosts. To quote Brigadier Zietsman again: "Like all guerrilla movements, they prefer to spread the activities over as wide an area as possible."

The 1976 national uprisings saw the exodus of more than 4,000 youths, many of whom joined the national liberation movements and rejuvenated them. But the changes in the balance of power in the South African subcontinent following the independence of Mozambique and Angola in 1975 and Zimbabwe in 1980 created favorable conditions for a symbiosis of the internally based existence and the externally based movements.

Pretoria's political ideologues responded to these developments by declaring that the country faced a total onslaught that was military, political, diplomatic, economic and psychological. This total onslaught, they argued, required a total strategy, the mobilization of the resources of the society for war.

While still chief of the defence forces, General Magnus Malan, the current Minister of Defence, explained the concept of total strategy as "the formulation of national objectives in which all the community's resources are mustered and managed on a co-ordinated level to ensure survival. Every activity of the state must be seen and understood as a function of total war."

Two key elements in military thinking about the future survival of the apartheid regime are the maintenance of a strong defence force and a commitment to domestic reform because, in the words of

Malan, "the solution to the problem in South Africa is only 20 per cent military and 80 per cent political."

An Afrikaner academic commented:

> Top generals believe that apartheid is still workable. Soweto needs tarred roads, bathtubs and electricity they say. Blacks think in terms of their basic human needs. Blacks don't think of political rights so they can bargain for these amenities.

Under P.W. Botha, the military has been able to consolidate its leadership within the white power structure so as to give effect to total strategy. The limited domestic reform that was part of total strategy included co-optation of the colored and Indian sections of the black community. Co-optation was to be effected through the creation of a tricameral parliament in which these two ethnic minorities would have limited jurisdiction over their own affairs.

In attempting to co-opt these two groups, the regime created legal space which was utilized to great effect by the anti-apartheid movement. The United Democratic Front, an umbrella organization of political organizations, community, youth and women's groups, was formed in 1983 to oppose the new constitution which created the tricameral parliament. It grew into the largest extra-parliamentary opposition, comprised of 700 affiliates with a total membership of approximately 3 million.

Black consciousness movements also campaigned against the regime's constitutional proposals and reform strategy. Mass protest reached new heights during 1984 to 1986. The final showdown appeared imminent. Blacks were more organized, militant and united than ever before, while whites were weaker, divided and on the retreat. The reality, however, was more complex.

Probably the most militarily powerful Third World regime was facing a popular rebellion of largely unarmed masses. By 1986 this conflict had reached stalemate. The state was militarily strong but politically weak while the popular movement and its leading representative, the ANC, was politically strong but militarily weak. Neither side had the combined military and political capacity to decisively seize the strategic initiative. Refusing to accept the inevitability of black rule, the regime declared a state of emergency in June 1986.

This gave the state a defensive shield for launching a new national security strategy aimed at "countering the revolutionary onslaught." Revolutions, to quote a senior military general, "are made by revolutionaries who exploit the grievances of the poor for their purposes." As a solution, the generals modified the low-intensity warfare strategies pursued by some Latin American regimes. This involved using extensive repression to eliminate the revolutionaries and massive socio-economic upgrading programs to deal with some black grievances.

By combining repression and reform, the regime hopes to dissipate the revolution. To manage this ambitious repressive reform program, a complex hierarchy of 400 security committees called joint management centres has been activated at national, regional and local levels. The committees, whose activities are secret, are chaired by military or police officials. So-called hard war sub-committees decide who is to be detained or killed and soft war sub-committees deal with welfare, economic and constitutional matters. Each township has a joint management centre that aims to achieve the right balance between hard and soft responses.

The overall strategic objective is to forcibly rip the black communities apart, extract and incarcerate the leadership kernel that helped organize them, and then to put the pieces together again on terms that leave white domination intact. The regime believes that it can outflank the liberation movement by rebuilding the communities in its own image.

By removing their base, the regime hopes to remove the need to negotiate with legitimate black leaders. Anti-apartheid organizations do not deny how damaging the state's ferocious retaliation has been. However, given that blacks remain politically disenfranchised, it is unlikely that the state's current strategy will achieve more than temporary compliance.

Black co-operation, not simply compliance, is the regime's deepest desire. But this will elude its grasp as long as the white minority refuses to accept the inevitability of democratic rule by a non-racial majority. In the interregnum, the white right wing has become increasingly prominent. This is not because more whites are voting for the right. Before 1987, the governing National Party faced a liberal official opposition in parliament. The crudely racist Conservative Party became the official opposition following its gains in the white general election of May 1987.

Conservative Party policies in 1987 were identical to National Party policies during the 1981 general election. The National Party moved fractionally leftward, in line with reform policies that conceded that black exclusion from the 1983 constitution was a mistake. The party split into two in 1982, leaving behind the Conservative Party and its loyalty to orthodox racism. One in two whites voted National Party in 1981, while one in four voted for the same policies in 1987, but this time espoused by the Conservative Party.

It is not the electorate that moved right, but the political parties that moved slightly leftward as they responded to black resistance. As resistance to apartheid in South Africa has increased, the Pretoria regime has introduced harsh new restrictions on the media, especially the print and electronic media.

Government action has been directed mainly at the alternative press, that is, the democratically structured grassroots or community supported newspapers which articulate the aspirations of the broad mass of people in their demands for a democratic society. Journalists have been detained without trial, subjected to torture and degrading treatment. Others have been assaulted by the police and their surrogates. Foreign journalists who have reported accurately on the unrest and police violence have been expelled from the country.

Aware that media coverage of unrest and police brutality helped galvanize international opposition to apartheid including the campaign for sanctions, the regime in 1985 and 1986 enacted stringent censorship laws under the state of emergency. Journalists are prohibited from scenes of unrest and from reporting on police action without ministerial approval.

In January 1987, following full-page advertisements in most newspapers marking the 75th anniversary of the ANC, the South African regime issued new regulations prohibiting advertisements in support of banned organizations. It also prohibited the media from quoting spokespersons of the ANC. When the new regulations were successfully challenged in the Natal provincial division of the Supreme Court, the regime hastily enacted new regulations to close the loopholes, thus preventing reporting of unrest in the townships.

This facilitated savage brutality against township residents by the security forces. In December 1987, new regulations aimed at the alternative media were gazetted. The Minister of Home Affairs and Information has been empowered to ban newspapers after three formal warnings. This legislation was used to shut down *New Nation*, *South* and *The Weekly Mail*. Similar action was recently taken against *Grassroots* and *New Era*. Other publications that face similar action are *Work In Progress* and *Saamstaan*. All these newspapers have been important in keeping the South African people informed of developments in their own country and in publicizing the democratic demands of the anti-apartheid movement.

South African police, for instance, confiscated copies of *The Weekly Mail* after the newspaper reported that 143 young white South Africans announced at a press conference that they would refuse to serve in the South African Defence Forces. In another recent action aimed at the alternative media, the regime announced — then under pressure rescinded — a decree requiring registration of all journalists and news agencies. A reason for the rescission of the registration requirement was the protest mounted nationally and internationally. In South Africa, the mass movement waged a *Hands off the Press* campaign that has been supported internationally. The work of the London-based organization, Article 19, and other organizations in exposing censorship and official harassment of journalists and other media workers in South Africa has been invaluable in mobilizing international support for the alternative media.

Suppression of the alternative media is analogous to killing the messenger. The root problems in South Africa will not be resolved until the government agrees to negotiate a settlement with the legitimate leaders, that is, those recognized and acknowledged by the mass of people as their leaders, rather than those chosen by the government. The mass of people have repeatedly stated that they recognize as their legitimate leaders, the leaders of the national liberation movements and those who have been incarcerated or forced into exile because of their commitment to the struggle for freedom.

The fundamental question in the future will be how a militarized white state uses co-optive strategies to achieve a critical mass of moderate black support. Can the white autocracy create a multiracial veneer to sell to the world?

The survival of radical black oppositions despite massive repression suggests the state's strategy will fail in the long run. In the end, genuine all-party negotiations will have to take place. Meanwhile violence, breakdown and degeneration will persist as the old order refuses to die and the new order struggles to be born.

It doesn't have to be a bloodbath. South Africa is a potentially normal country.

"This is not a catastrophe that was destined to happen. This is something that was buggered up by people behaving badly that could be repaired by people behaving well."

By Gwynne Dyer

I scarcely know what to say. I sat wondering what on earth I could usefully contribute to the proceedings. I worked in South Africa, certainly, but I can't even get into the country anymore. I get refused visas regularly, and if you are a freelance journalist with no organization behind you, forget it. NBC can twist arms. I can't.

And there's not a lot I can dare say about censorship. I can write about what I like about South Africa, and indeed many South African newspapers publish my column, but I can't go there anymore. I've been dealt with. So I was feeling rather fifth-wheel to the proceedings. And then Heribert Adam got up during the question period this morning and said something that triggered something in my head. He said, "Please don't talk about black majority rule. It is the wrong phrase to use. Talk about majority rule."

And I thought, "Oh, God, he's got me there. I've been using the phrase for years." And, of course, he is absolutely right. We're not talking about black majority rule. Yes, there is a black majority in South Africa. But we're not talking about black rule over white. We're talking about majority rule. That's what should occur in South Africa.

Gwynne Dyer writes a twice-weekly column on international affairs. It appears in about 150 newspapers in 30 countries. He has published two books — *War*, in collaboration with Tina Viljoen, and *The Defence of Canada*. Dyer's professional involvement in covering South Africa dates from the early 1970s, and he has considerable experience working there. He holds a PhD in military and Middle Eastern history from the University of London. He has taught at the Canadian Forces College in Toronto and the Royal Military Academy at Sandhurst, England.

Don't use that phrase, "black majority rule," because it implies exactly what the South African government would have you believe — which is that any change will be to a different but equally reprehensible system of oppression, which I don't think we should buy into.

Then I started to hear a couple of other magic words. "Objectivity" was one, and "context-setting" was the other. Now we've all been through this before, I know. But I guess I ought to fly my colors openly. The myth of objectivity is both a myth, and a necessity for a working journalist. Of course, objectivity is a myth. You select your facts according to your interpretation of what is important. You are therefore setting a context.

On the other hand, if you are of my persuasion, you attempt not to do it in accord with some preconceived ideology, but with at least fairly frequent contact with the reality in the streets. But context-setting is the central part of the job. You are setting context. You might as well admit it. You are not doing it as a propagandist. We all deny that we are crusaders.

But we are setting context, and we might as well admit it. Some people do it quite explicitly. For example, every story that comes out on the wire services now has got the standard paragraphs about two-thirds of the way through the story, that tell everybody what they should know about the country, right?

Today in South Africa this too happens, and about two-thirds of the way down through the story, it says South Africa is a country where five million whites exercise political power over 25 million blacks who don't have a vote. Associated Press (AP), United Press International (UPI), they all do it. There's a standard paragraph in there. That's context-setting. So what ought we be doing in terms of context-setting for people who don't pay regular and constant attention to it? — people who ultimately have some influence on the outcome, because they elect governments that have either this policy or that, outside South Africa.

There are several principal alternative futures for South Africa which we might influence. One of them is not the great and bloody revolution that brings liberation in the new day. That will never happen. Anybody who knows South Africa knows that the balance of power in force within a country will never allow the clean kill, as they say. The one alternative is that South Africa gradually, and it may be happening already, slides into a perpetual gigantic Lebanon. I mean, no clean solution, no solution ever, but an escalating level of violence and increasing prevalence with no-go zones — just an awful slide into perpetual, low-level civil war, which is an awful thing for a country that deserves better.

The alternative solution, which one has to squeeze one's eyes tightly closed and take a deep breath and believe very hard in, is that South Africa can become what it ought to be. What it ought to have been all along, which is a modern and industrialized, civilized, prosperous country with majority rule, in which most people are black, but whites still have a home, a place, a role in the society, are accepted in South Africa. You do have to squeeze your eyes tightly shut right now, but that's what I'm talking about, context-setting.

It is within the constraints of objectivity, of not distorting the present. How can we set context when we talk about South Africa in such a way that we influence the outcome towards the latter rather then the former alternative. The very first time I went to South Africa, in the early 1970s, I flew into Johannesburg. I arrived in South Africa having had it drilled into me by every South African I had ever met, that stupid North American that I was, I ought not believe that South Africa is like the American South. South Africa is different.

And so you arrive in South Africa having been seriously drilled on the idea that South Africa is a unique place for which there are no analogies from your experience. And I got out of the airplane, went through the customs, got my rented car and started driving into Johannesburg, and the very first thing you do is you punch up the radio stations. And I got first of all South African Broadcasting Corporation (SABC), English-Afrikaans service, which was like a time warp from BBC home service in the 1950s, though this was the early 1970s.

Then I hit the African stations. And the thing that struck me right away, and I know this is simplistic, except it was confirmed by a lot of subsequent experience, was that I could be listening to Detroit FM rock stations. You've been lying to me all this time. This is not in fact all that different. And everything I know about South Africa from that day to this, tells me, that although, yes, of course, a great deal about South Africa is different, as every country is different from any other. Something coming over the radio is just an indication that maybe things ain't like what you were told they were. But a lot of subsequent experience has told me the same. South Africa is a normal country — normal in the sense of the industrialized, prosperous democratic world. It has all of those potentials in it, gone wrong, rather than a country that could never have been that.

South Africa is a country that could, with majority rule, not black majority rule, work as Canada works, as Sweden works, as Spain works, as Greece works. At the very worst, as Greece works, which ain't bad compared to how it is now. The present in South Africa was not inevitable, and neither is the future that we envisage simply by extrapolating the present.

Things are as they are now because bad decisions were made in the past, not because it was written in the stars. Let me give you just one example. You hear in South Africa about how it would be all right to have majority rule if only there was a big black middle class that had an interest in the investment in the society, and would act as a sort of ballast on political opinion and provide moderate political leadership to the black Marxists.

Well, in a way I'm not sure that doesn't actually exist. But to the extent that it isn't as big as it ought to be or might have been, has got to do with the decisions that were made after 1948, when essentially the entire Afrikaner working class and sub-working class were boot-strapped into the middle class by government action, instead of allowing enterprising blacks to get in there.

This is why South Africa is run by something like 40 per cent of Afrikaners who work for the government. These are actual political decisions that were made, rather than what had to happen. Good decisions, the right decisions, the brave decisions, could restore normality — normality in the sense that I have been talking about.

South Africa can be, with a little bit of luck and a lot of intelligence and some courage, a country that isn't all that different from Canada, or at least Greece or Argentina at the very worst, without the coups, in terms of how people live. Now that ain't bad, compared to the way it is for most people who live there now. It can have majority rule and the rule of law, and peace and even prosperity, if the right decisions are made.

It's late, and I don't think it's too late. Now in terms of context, in terms of how journalists can deal with that perspective if they wanted its deep background in most stories; it never in fact features in the story at all. It's a set of assumptions you approach the subject with — which conditions, how you write, rather than what you write. But I do think that it's important to make the assumption that South Africa is not a disaster that had to happen, which cannot be prevented or diverted from its forwarding course.

It's a potentially normal country, and I know I'm using normal in a special sense, but it's our sense. A potentially normal country gone wrong because of political decisions, and could be brought back to that kind of normality by other political decisions. That's a context that could make a tremendous difference to the way people write about South Africa, the way people treat South Africa in film. It doesn't mean one does different things, covers different stories. It's a question of how you treat it.

It won't make you more beloved by the government, by the way. And this is not something that's going to make the government happy, though at first glance one might think so. In fact, it doesn't.

I think the question of perspective is vital. Without being a Pollyanna, I think that it is quite important to express this possibility that South Africa, by taking the right decisions, by having the courage to take the chances, can become a civilized, reasonable, prosperous, democratic, peaceful country.

I don't honestly know if that is still possible. I think it is still possible. I know it's less possible than if that process had begun 10 years ago. A lot of time has been wasted. But I think that it's important to believe that it is at least still possible. If you don't imagine the future you want, it is very unlikely that you will like the future you get. And that is true about the way we deal with South Africa as well.

It's not a question of describing wonderful futures for South Africa, which nobody can do without breaking down into tears at the moment. It is important to hold in one's mind, as one addresses any questions about South Africa, the idea that this is not a catastrophe that was destined to happen. This is something that was buggered up by people behaving badly that could be repaired by people behaving well. And although I won't offer precise prescriptions for how one deals with that in any media, you hold it in the back of your mind, and it does condition the way you approach the story.

2

Being a Journalist in South Africa

Frustration, censorship, harassment, threats and imprisonment are daily problems for those who try to report the real story in South Africa. Six journalists tell what it's like working in the media and engaging in the battle to preserve what's left of press freedom.

Phillip van Niekerk
Freelancer, *The Globe and Mail*

Anton Harber
Co-editor of *The Weekly Mail*

Ameen Akhalwaya
Editor of *The Indicator*

Max du Preez
Editor of *Vrye Weekblad*

Thami Mazwa
Senior Editor of *The Sowetan*

Harvey Tyson
Editor-In-Chief of *The Johannesburg Star*

South Africa's press stands on the edge of a new frontier, says a former *Rand Daily Mail* staff member.

"A new mainstream press, more representative of all South Africa's people, is starting to emerge."

By Phillip van Niekerk

In opening this panel on being a journalist in South Africa, I want to move away for an instant from victimology, that is, a practice of restating the long litany of cruel and very repressive abuses sponsored or permitted by the South African government.

This is not because journalists in South Africa do not have major cause to be depressed about the future of their profession, but because for once there is also some cause for optimism.

Journalism today in South Africa stands on the edge of a new frontier. Only a few years back, virtually all the media, the English press, the Afrikaans press, and the broadcasting media were in the group of monopolies — Monopolies not only of ownership, but monopolies of ideas.

For years I worked on what was characterized as the liberal English-language press of South Africa. Professional frustrations of my contemporaries and I were ongoing and destructive. It was an inherent conservatism, a fear of alienating white readers. We had to struggle to get the activities of the extra-parliamentary black political and labor movements into the paper at all, and they were very seldom on the front page.

Phillip van Niekerk has worked for many South African publications, including the *Daily Dispatch* (East London), the *Cape Times (*Cape Town) and the *Rand Daily Mail* (Johannesburg). He has specialized in squatter settlements around Cape Town, the black trade union movement and black labor in the goldmines. Van Niekerk is a freelance contributor for the *Toronto Globe and Mail* and *The Weekly Mail* in Johannesburg. In 1988-89 he was a visiting fellow at the Centre of Press, Politics and Public Policy at Harvard University's Kennedy School of Government.

It was particularly frustrating for my black colleagues to be eternally relegated to the township beat, writing as if from a foreign land for unsympathetic white editors who regarded the middle-class suburban perspective of the world as unchallengeable.

When *The Rand Daily Mail* closed down in April 1985, it was an incredibly sad day for many of us. But those of us who were on it at the end knew that all that was left by 1985 was a skeleton of its former self after all the meat had been thrown to the crocodiles.

In retrospect, the death of *The Mail* was an important turning point for the press in South Africa. New publications not owned by the Anglo-American Corporation or the government began to move into the void of critical journalism in South Africa. The *Weekly Mail, South, Indicator, Saamstaan* and *New Nation,* were launched in this period. They were all voices which transcended the all-star liberal notions that reform would come from parliament.

They were born at a time of civil conflict in South Africa in the mid '80s. Their contribution was to report on and to varying degrees to promote the aspirations of the people who were deprived of the constitutional vote for fighting the government in the streets. Not only did these publications set out to expose the repression of the security forces, but they represented ideas which were deeply threatening to the government and the ruling establishment.

When the second emergency was declared in June 1986, the media were one of the prime targets. During this time, the eyes of state became a threat to state security.

For many journalists this has meant jail and banning. The more outlying the area, the greater the struggle for information and the more unrestrained the behavior of the authorities.

With tiny circulation and resources, the alternative press have become more relevant to the history of my country than the owners of *The Rand Daily Mail*, who had closed down because they thought there was no place in the market for a newspaper that sold to black and white readers at the same time. Instead, that company, Times Media Limited, looks increasingly belligerent and reactionary, dominated by wealthy white male executives who believe that anything less than worshipful adoration of the free market means you are a dangerous left-winger.

These people, with all their power and money, are moving to the margins. And a new mainstream press, more representative of all South Africa's people, is starting to emerge.

The alternative press is an important catalyst in this change, for one can not ignore the black press — publications such as *City Press* in Soweto, which preceded them and for so long were treated as inferior cousins to the white press. Hopefully in time labels such as alternative and white and black press will become redundant.

Some of the large-circulation mainstream papers supported the alternative newspapers during the state's attacks on them, refusing to allow the government to drive a wedge between them which would have left papers such as the *Weekly Mail* and *New Nation* even more isolated and vulnerable. And these publications, such as the *Star* in Johannesburg and the *Natal Witness* in Pietermaritzburg are also part of this melting pot of change.

The dangerous past lies in the way of South African journalists. There is still stultifying censorship that would drive most western journalists to howl with fury, and the survival of a critical press for the alternative media is far from where it should be. Indeed the frontier may turn out to be a precipice.

But if in the rough times ahead the press can survive the attacks on itself, the debate over what kind of a press, over what kind of a society, over what kind of a democracy we want, is only just beginning.

Foreign support is vital to the survival of the alternative press, says the co-editor of one of South Africa's leading opposition papers.

"You have to have the street fighter's desire to spill blood on the streets, I'm afraid, and get involved in scraps on street corners rather than in the courts."

By Anton Harber

I would like to tell you how important it is to a paper like ours to have international contact. When our paper was threatened with closure in October 1988, our sentence was reduced, suddenly and inexplicably, from three months to one month. I am certain that a key factor in the reduction of that sentence, and a key factor in the survival of the paper, was the amount of international attention and pressure that was brought to bear. So it is really very important to us to have this kind of contact, to know that there are people who are concerned.

In the five or six days I have been out of South Africa, the first or the second question people ask, after the one about Winnie Mandela, is how things are going at *The Weekly Mail.* And I found myself saying in the first few days, "Well, in fact we're feeling quite good. We're feeling quite strong. We came back from our closure with good sales. We lost less advertising than we feared we'd lose. It's been relatively quiet since then, so that's why I can be in London or Canada and get away."

But then suddenly I realized what I was saying, and I actually sat down and wrote a list of what has happened since our closure and a brief description of our current situation, and I realized how ludicrous

Anton Harber worked as a political reporter at *The Rand Daily Mail.* When it closed in 1985, he and other journalists started *The Weekly Mail,* an alternative newspaper. Its right to publish was temporarily suspended by the government in October 1988. He is co-editor of the paper, based in Johannesburg. Harber has been vice-president of the SA Society of Journalists, an executive member of the Anti-Censorship Action Group, and was a joint winner of the Pringle Award for Press Freedom in 1987.

it was. One edition of our newspaper was seized, taken off the streets, in August. That was the second time it happened to us, and that can happen to us at any time. It can happen as our paper hits the streets again on Friday. I'm sure it will happen again at some stage. We were closed for a month in November. That leaves you in a situation, once you've been closed, of being on two weeks' notice. It simply takes a letter from the Minister to give one two weeks to make representations to him, and one can be closed thereafter with very little recourse to the courts or anything else.

Since the beginning of the year, we have had four police visits, each one investigated an allegation of a contravention of either the emergency regulations or the *Police Act* or one of the many other acts we have to keep our eyes on as journalists in South Africa.

In January, my co-editor's home was fire-bombed. I don't know if it was aimed at him or at the newspaper. He has a brother who is a prominent human rights lawyer. But the point is that his home was fire-bombed, which you can say was a pretty extreme form of censorship. Our newspaper and myself are facing a libel action from the Minister of Home Affairs. He's suing us for 50,000 rand for a description I gave of him right after he closed our newspaper. I have countered with a libel suit against the Minister for a description that he gave of us just after he closed our newspaper. We also have at least one threat of what we call a 205, a subpoena forcing a journalist to name a source.

I don't give this list because I want to indulge in victimology. I just want to bring home the point that when answering the question about how things were going, a few days ago I was able to brush aside these things I considered normal and routine. I thought it was a quiet period, and it was a quiet period. I think this brings home the extraordinary level of direct and indirect violence, of threats, of attacks that we put up with on a day-to-day basis. Each one of these things, as recently as 18 months to two years ago, would have been a major problem and a major worry. But even taken together now, I consider that they're routine.

I was looking through a list of events related to censorship put out by a group called the Anti-Censorship Action Group. It lists about 25 incidents during the month of February. That brings home how much we've got used to under the state of emergency as it approaches the end of its third year. I suppose one reason we consider it quiet is because we have the sense that things are not going to get better; they're only going to get worse. One has to learn to live with these kinds of things, as horrifying as they may be.

But also there is a sense that after almost three years of emergency, I don't know how, I don't know why, but we have survived, and therefore we have learned to live with it. It's important to realize that when it comes to censorship in South Africa, we concentrate on the emergency, quite naturally now, but censorship takes many forms. The oppression under the emergency is just the most recent and the most severe. I'd like to run through a few of the others, just to give a broad picture of the kinds of problems that we face.

There is pre-emergency law — normal law written in the statute books and of which the list on South Africa is so long it would be impossible to run through. The most vicious of those laws are the *Prisons Act, the Police Act, the Defence Act* and *the Energy Act.* There is a whole list of them, all of which are severe, and all of which even before the emergency led us to say often that we didn't have a free press, and that it was very severely restricted — restricted more than in most comparable countries.

The situation was very serious even before the emergency. But if that situation had any virtue, it was that those were laws, they were statutes, which meant they could be tested in court. One didn't always have access to courts, and could be detained without trial, and newspapers could be closed without access to courts, but by and large, when those laws were implemented, one had a chance to go to court and defend oneself, even if the law was unfair, even if the courts were unjust.

For papers like mine, a key element in fighting censorship is financial. The papers we are talking about are small, young, uncapitalized, underfinanced and always short of money. They survive mostly by finding printers who extend long credit and bank managers who have a degree of tolerance. It's very difficult to keep advertisers when our paper is on two weeks' notice of closure and can be seized without any notice at all. We have found that whenever there is a threat to papers like ours, advertisers just flee for the door. That's the last we ever see of them.

Obviously this affects things like subscriptions, the life blood of a paper like mine. It's very difficult to convince people to put up money for six months or a year or two years for a paper with an uncertain and unpredictable future.

There is also a very severe shortage of good, skilled, trained journalists equipped to handle the alternative press, the new newspapers, the kinds of diverse work they have to do. It's not simply a case of being a journalist. It's being administrator, distributor, advertising salesperson, and conference speaker.

Another problem papers like ours face is the monopoly in the newspaper industry in South Africa. A couple of companies, one in the English press and one in the Afrikaans press, dominate the major weekly and daily titles. All the large daily English-language papers in all the major cities and most of the minor cities are controlled by the Argus Company, and this creates enormous problems for young, smaller papers like ours. These companies control not just newspaper titles but printing, distribution, a good deal of the paper industry. We have to print our paper at Springs, a tiny place 45 minutes outside Johannesburg, which causes us enormous deadline problems and costs us much more. We recently decided one way to deal with this was to try to get a simultaneous press run in Cape Town, which is our second major selling area. There are two printing presses in Cape Town that could handle a print run of this sort. One is owned by National Press, the National Party-supporting Afrikaans newspaper industry. They declined to even give us a quote for the job. The other is owned by the Argus Company, which said they had no time to print our newspaper. We're stuck with printing in Springs, and unable to print in Cape Town.

It has become clear in recent months that censorship has increasingly taken an extra-legal form, and is operating informally, outside of the law. The firebomb I told you about earlier is a worrying development, particularly in the context of a series of bombs aimed at anti-apartheid people, the churches, the trade unions and so on. Then there is the frequency that South African Airways manages to forget to fly our newspaper around the country and delivers it a day or two days later. And of course there is detention without trial, and restriction orders faced by editors like Zwelakhe Sisulu, which prevents him from doing his work.

And then one comes to the emergency regulations themselves. They are the most immediate and major concern to all the papers, and particularly the alternative press. What the emergency has meant is a complex succession of regulations over a period of almost three years. During this time, the regulations have gradually been broken down as the newspapers have gathered strength and courage to take on the regulations and to find loopholes and grey areas. They have been vigorous and rigorous in finding those greys areas, exploiting them and challenging them in court. This has led the government to bring in new regulations, tighten up old, and close those grey areas.

The process of closing *The Weekly Mail* for one month came after an 11-month-long series of warnings, representations, gazetted warnings, official warnings, unofficial warnings, arguments and discussions. They threatened us constantly.

The three years of the state of the emergency have changed the nature of censorship fundamentally. I said earlier that one of the virtues of pre-emergency law was that usually you had a chance to argue your case in court. This meant that the decision you were making would be,"Do I have a legal defence" and "Are they going to prosecute?" and "Do I have a reasonable chance of defending myself in court?" Even in the beginning of the emergency, the regulations were much vaguer. The question asked was, "If I get prosecuted for breaking an emergency regulation, will I be able to defend myself in court? Do I have a strong argument? What is the lawyer's advice on that?" And the lawyer would essentially put up a percentage on your chances of acquittal, or at least of putting up a good defence.

What has happened under the emergency regulations with the power to seize and the power to close newspapers is that no one has access to the court. It's not a question of how strong the defence is. The power to seize and close lies arbitrarily with one person. A paper can be seized if a middle-ranking policeman decides there is a contravention of the emergency. The two times we've been seized, we tried to get him to prove it in court, and failed.

The power to close newspapers lies with the Minister of Home Affairs, who is not known (and I must be careful because I already have one lawsuit against me,) for his high level of literacy. One man is in control, and has created a pretence of legality, by giving papers the right to make representations to him, but I think our own experience shows just how much this is a pretence.

When we got our first warning in December 1987, we spent three weeks with the legal team doing up a 180 pages of argument to put to him. We took it very seriously. We spent a lot of money, a lot of time, and we put it to him. By the time we got to our final stage of warning last October it was clear that the process was just a pretence and we had no more than a token right to make legal representation. We didn't want to give the system credibility by taking it too seriously, so we prepared a token response. We said, in effect, "Look, we don't actually believe you're going to read this and that it's going to mean anything, but if you want to hear our arguments, read what we wrote in 180 pages 10 months ago." As far as we could determine, he never even read our 180 pages.

South African censorship has always had a bizarre or alien character. Perhaps the best illustration of this is the *Key Points Act*, which says you cannot take photographs, describe, draw, sketch or do a whole lot of things in relation to a key point. And we ask ourselves, "Well, what is a key point?" If I tell people what a key point is, the ANC would know what they should be bombing. But the government won't tell us what the key points are, so we are in this bizarre situation where we can't take pictures of things that we don't know what they are. So you find out eventually — when prosecuted and found guilty.

Things have reached an extreme stage under the state of emergency because it's arbitrary law, because you don't have a chance to defend yourself in court, and it really depends on the whims of people, and their whims change and the rules change. We've always had a system in South Africa of enforced self-censorship. Rather than putting the censor in the office, they just lay down the perimeters and tell you, "If you exceed the perimeters of what you may or may not publish, you will be punished," but essentially, the decision of whether or not you're going to exceed it rests with you.

Under the emergency everybody knows there are those perimeters, but nobody actually knows where they are. We have talked with the Minister, with his lackeys, with all sorts of people, and we've never been able to find out where they are. We also know that if we find out where they are, the Minister can wake up one morning and change them, since it's purely at will. That's an impossible situation to deal with.

It means essentially that whereas previously, we developed legal strategies to deal with censorship in South Africa. Now we rely primarily on political strategies. We rely on building up our political support locally and internationally. Since we don't have access to the courts to defend ourselves, we put pressure on the government to stop action against us, by building up arguments and political organizations and anti-censorship groups.

The lawyers are being replaced by street fighters. At the beginning of the emergency, every journalist had to be an expert on the law, and the lawyers spent an enormous amount of time in the office. Now the advice one really needs is not advice on what is or isn't legal, but on what one can or cannot get away with — how far one can push the local policeman before he hits you back. You have to have the street fighter's desire to spill blood on the streets, I'm afraid, and get involved in scraps on street corners rather than in the courts.

The old strategies have to be changed. We're thrashing around in the dark looking for the perimeters of what we can or cannot do, constantly trying to push them back, but not knowing quite where they are. It may be fairly relaxed this week, but next week the paper can be seized, next week the perimeters can narrow, next week the Minister can change his mind about what he likes and doesn't like.

When he does give reasons for action against the newspaper, they're contradictory. They're inexplicable. He allows some papers to do certain things which he doesn't allow others to do. He allows you to do something this week which he doesn't allow next week. It's impossible to know why our paper was not so severe a threat to the security of the state that people could buy it and read it in October, but that wasn't the case in November and suddenly it became again the case in December that it wasn't such a severe threat.

I want to deal with one other issue. The coverage of the Winnie Mandela story has raised questions as difficult and problematic and tortuous as the story itself. These are important issues for papers like ours, which are trying to address what's the most appropriate kind of press for a changing South Africa. What level of independence is appropriate?

Some papers, mainstream and alternative, have simply ignored or gone very low key on the controversy around Winnie Mandela and her football team. After difficult discussions, arguments, consultations, and a long process of thought, my paper decided to break the story and to cover it as fully as we could. This has raised the issue of what kind of journalism is appropriate for a newspaper like ours, which is new and young and attempting to develop a journalism appropriate to a new and different South Africa.

The question one has to ask is: Should we, as we've traditionally done, just be aiming our criticisms and our probing at the state, the forces of apartheid and its supporters? Or is it also our role to probe and query and criticize what's happening in the resistance movement, in the liberation forces and opposition organizations?

When we have a story like this, which presents major problems for the resistance movement, do we cover it or do we cover it up? Do we simply do what the resistance movement tells us to do, or is there space for a more independent position? What does one do when the resistance movement cannot give you clear direction, when some members are saying one should cover the story, and others are saying one should cover it up?

It's a very difficult and important question. Is there a role for an independent critical press in South Africa today, and will there be one in the future? What a paper like ours is trying to say is that there is a role, and that the appropriate kind of journalism for a changing and a changed South Africa is not a journalism that is subservient to any particular organization or any particular individual, but is independent and critical and probes and asks the questions and causes controversy.

The Afrikaans press has been entirely subservient to the National Party, and that makes us wary of accepting a position where one is totally subservient to particular organizations or individuals. But having said that, I don't think in South Africa one can proclaim a simple, principled independence. It's a complex and difficult conflict and creates a lot of dilemmas for journalism, and certainly for our paper, which is a campaigning newspaper, a paper with a point of view. One has to balance the need to pursue change against the danger of becoming entirely subservient to a particular organizations involved in change.

There used to be a simple distinction in South African journalism between objectivity and subjectivity. And there used to be a simple argument between those who said newspapers must be objective and independent, and those who said you have to choose sides, and once you've chosen a side, that's where you've got to stand. The first of those arguments was discredited by its abuse, by the lack of objectivity among those who proclaimed it the strongest. And the argument that one simply has to choose sides and stay there is no longer enough.

I believe we have to develop a journalism where one does take sides, one is fighting for change, but where one is not merely subservient to organizations, and can maintain a level of independence.

"Media guerrillas" counter the official violence of the state by shooting back with their only weapons — words.

"We are involved in a cat and mouse game."

By Ameen Akhalwaya

Winston Churchill was an old colonialist and racist. I didn't think very much of him, but he had a marvelous way with words. In the House of Commons once, he castigated his opponents, saying, "Half of them are liars." The speaker pointed out it was unparliamentary to call honorable members liars, and asked him to retract. "I'm sorry," Churchill reportedly said. "Half of them are not liars."

I use this anecdote to illustrate in a nutshell the conflict between the government and the so-called alternative media in South Africa. We are trying to counteract, to put into perspective the half-truths, the partial truths and the untruths of officialdom. In fact another Churchillian phrase comes to mind, that of "terminological inexactitude." That probably sums up better how, in the wake of ever-increasing curbs on reporting what the government regards as subversive statements, we try to get the essential message across.

For the noose on reporting political activism has been tightening since the 1950s, when it was aimed specifically at smaller left-wing publications which were later banned altogether, and the liberal *Rand Daily Mail*, which was on the point of strangling the more serious newspapers.

Ameen Akhalwaya is a political columnist for *Post Natal* and a correspondent for South in Cape Town and *Africa Report* in New York. He was the first black political reporter to work on *The Rand Daily Mail*. In 1985 he was instrumental in launching *The Indicator,* the first of the alternative newspapers set up in South Africa after *The Rand Daily Mail* and *Sunday Express* closed.

In this battle for survival, writing for and editing serious newspapers has become a frustrating, but at the same time, a challenging task. Sometimes on our own, sometimes aping more daring mainstream newspapers, sometimes with the aid of lawyers, we are involved in a cat and mouse game, of beating the government's conspiracy of deception.

An example of this was in Lenasia, which is a group area adjacent to Soweto. Amichand Rajbansi, who until recently was one of two darkies in Botha's cabinet, before he was booted out in disgrace, came to address a public meeting at the Civic Centre, which is directly across the road from our offices. About 150 people were in the hall to listen, so we thought, to the man regarded by the government as the leader of those in South Africa who are classified Indian. Clearly the community shunned him, for United Democratic Front affiliates, those opposed to the government, had consistently drawn up to 2,000 people to their rallies at the same place.

But what was more intriguing was the scene outside the hall. There were all sorts of vehicles, some seemingly private, but mostly security force vehicles. There was a huge contingent of armed men around the hall, and our lawyers had told us at the time that it was illegal, under the emergency regulations, to identify security forces and to report on boycott actions.

But inside the hall, militant students made up the majority of the audience of 150. As soon as Rajbansi walked on to the stage, the students rose. Everyone thought that he was going to get a standing round of applause, but instead they walked out as a form of protest, which they could not do legally outside. They could not demonstrate outside.

Rajbansi claimed to an ever-credible white press that more than 400 people had been in the hall. We wrote a story saying that figure might have been right if "all those unidentified armed men outside the hall were taken into account." Now our readers got the message: one, that there was a protest against the cabinet minister: two, the community boycotted his meeting; three, a large contingent of security forces had to protect him, and this is a so-called leader and a clever militant.

The readers had to read between the lines, of course, but more than that, the authorities knew what we had done. We indulged in much self-congratulation. We cheered our ingenuity. But we knew that it was just another little pyrrhic victory. Sure enough, a policeman called me later to say it was clear we had been too clever by half in circumventing the regulations, but we should be warned that loopholes in the regulations would be closed. The government came up with a devastating retaliation. The Minister of Home Affairs could suspend newspapers from publishing for long periods.

His decision, he admitted, might be subjective, but so long as he followed the proper procedure in warning and then suspending the offending newspaper, he need give no reason. Thus the courts were effectively barred from overturning his decree. The Minister, in fact, called those of us in the emerging press "media terrorists". We were actually quite offended by that. In terms of the Churchillian quote that I mentioned earlier, we regard ourselves as media guerrillas

We counter the official violence of the state by shooting back with our only weapon — words. But we are forced to spend much more time walking, as a South African leader once said, "blindfolded in a mine field". It has reached such a stage that as editors, we all probably spend much more time discussing how to avoid being blown up in that mine field than in the normal exercise of editorial duties. For some of us on smaller, hopelessly under-staffed newspapers, it is no exaggeration to say that about 60 per cent of our time is spent on non-editorial activities such as keeping our financial accounts in order, avoiding bank managers and so on.

But why do we carry on? And should we carry on? Well, in the late '70s and early '80s, senior black journalists thought long and hard about our roles. More especially, whether we should carry on amid all the restrictions, and they were less severe then, and whether we should be involved in telling readers only part of the truth. We were more concerned about our credibility. People in black townships saw what was happening, and sometimes reports of incidents bore a distinct dissimilarity to what they had witnessed.

Often those who worked on newspapers run by whites found little sympathy about reporting what was going on in the black townships. There were and still are precious few newspapers prepared to rock the boat in South Africa. In fact, my experience was that whenever a controversial story about black politics was written, there was a knee-jerk reaction from white sub-editors, who insisted without even reading the story that it be submitted to lawyers for clearance.

We find that pretty ludicrous, but the truth is that the regulations haven't affected most of them. They've had very little effect in black areas in any case. Instead of giving in, black journalists and indeed some very courageous white journalists, who knew their bosses were copping out, decided to go their own way, to start their own newspapers. Another reason for going it alone, of course, was that black journalists on white newspapers ran into a racist wall. We were shunted backwards and sideways and fobbed off with claims that we were being promoted.

The bosses also claimed that black journalists, because of their commitment to writing from the so-called liberation perspective, couldn't be trusted to be objective. Not that any newspaper, least of all in South Africa, can be totally objective. The best we can try for is balance. But the cry by black journalists that committed journalism did not mean bending the facts was ignored. And even now, people in the establishment media who should know better accuse the "alternative" press of bending facts, but they don't produce the evidence.

In my experience the reverse is often true. The establishment newspapers bend the truth when it suits them. Many instances are distorted by omission. For example, they will publish soccer results from Albania and Yugoslavia and other seemingly exotic places from their vantage point, but they don't even bother to publish the results of an organization known as the South African Council on Sports, otherwise known as Sacos. When Sacos does feature occasionally in the white press, it is usually for the purpose of being attacked for its political stance. Why? Because Sacos regards itself as part of the liberation struggle. It refuses to play what passes for non-racial sport in an abnormal South African society and is a champion of South Africa's total sports isolation.

Obviously, white sportswriters, robbed of the glory of covering recognized international events, retaliate by blotting out Sacos from the white public altogether.

I resigned from *The Rand Daily Mail*, the most concerned and sympathetic white newspaper that black South Africans have ever had, because I was "promoted" to a new post which carried a fancy title, a big salary and little worthwhile to write about. I was told that the paper was trying to appeal to "the southern suburbs housewife" and that my type of writing would alienate the poor white housewife. Noteworthy is the fact that the truth of our articles were never in dispute.

That's when we decided to launch *The Indicator* as a free-sheet newspaper in the relatively affluent black community with a relatively well-educated audience. When I talk about black, I'm talking about those who have been identified as so-called Indian and so-called African in all the official terms, which is now called black. It used to be called Bantu and various other things.

First, we wanted to fill the void left by the liberal decline and subsequent closure of *The Rand Daily Mail* in providing serious articles of interest to black readers. Incidentally, *The Rand Daily Mail's* readership was 72 per cent black. Second, we wanted to play an educational role, explaining the various issues that affected not only people in our area of distribution but also regionally and nationally. Third, we wanted to counteract the government's conspiracy of deception by trying to show events from a different perspective — the perspective of the victims of apartheid. Fourth, and most importantly, we wanted to provide a platform for those who needed it most but were unable to get it in the mainstream press. And fifth, we did not see ourselves as an alternative, but rather as complementary to the major newspapers.

But the truth is that none of the emerging papers has the financial or staff resources to challenge the major groups in terms of their range of editorial services. We look to newspapers such as *The Star*, which has tried very hard, under very difficult circumstances, to reflect what is going on in the black communities. Often *The Star* has tested the regulations to the limit and we have followed its lead simply because we cannot afford the huge fees for consulting lawyers daily.

Lawyers are crucial in our approach. In this regard we have been very fortunate. Our lawyers have charged us very little and at times nothing. The lawyers told us very honestly, I thought, that we knew the regulations as well as they did, but they didn't find anything subversive in our interpretation or their definition of what was written. But as they pointed out, the types of stories we concentrated on were the very ones the government found offensive and there was no saying how the Minister in his subjective opinion would view it. So they advised us to carry on as we did without always consulting them. Only in extreme cases or in matters such as possible libel do we now consult them.

An excellent example of this mixed-up situation came to light. The leader of the Pan-Africanist Congress in 1987, Zaph Mothopeng, was released unconditionally from jail. The PAC, like the ANC and several other organizations, is banned. We cannot write anything that would further its aims or that would enhance the standing of the organization. All the same, I conducted a lengthy interview with Mr. Mothopeng. *The Indicator* ran the interview in full, because it was important that the views of a leader of a major organization be aired, debated and challenged in public. I cut out just one line where he said, "The colonizers had raped Azania." I did so because I felt this was the type of view that the authorities would use as an excuse to clobber us.

The article was offered to three other newspapers — two black-edited papers belonging to a major white newspaper group, and a so-called alternative newspaper. The two black-edited newspapers in cities 200 kilometres apart submitted the article to their respective lawyers. Independently the lawyers concurred that nearly 40 per cent of the interview should be cut or modified, including the word "Azania". They thought that would offend the Minister. One of the editors decided to comply with the lawyer's suggestion. The interview made little sense. The other editor decided the article was not subversive, over-ruled his lawyer's suggestion, and ran it in full.

The so-called alternative newspaper cut the interview probably for reasons of space. But the important thing is that the government didn't react. The incident showed exactly how difficult it is to know what is and what isn't acceptable. But equally importantly, we were accused by radical opponents of the PAC of being PAC supporters because we had given Mr. Mothopeng so much space. Ironically, the police and the opponents of the ANC accuse us of being a front for the ANC.

This accusation over the Mothopeng article needs to be seen in context too, for black censorship works at different levels. Black journalists and those in the emerging press, and I'm sure the white journalists now as well, are under pressure not only from the government but also from extra-parliamentary activists. Some groups have taken it upon themselves to label journalists and the emerging newspapers as being members of one or the other rival ideological group, to be shunned or boycotted if they are not kosher.

In one instance, a newspaper was targeted for boycott by a major group because it ran an article which allegedly confirmed that newspaper's ideological bias. The article had also been published in a white newspaper. Far from the boycott succeeding, that newspaper's circulation soared to unprecedented levels because, I suspect, people wanted to see if it was as bad as it was painted. Of great concern, of course, is that many of our leaders who are loud in denouncing the government's censorship are deafeningly silent in condemning their own supporters' attempts. When we launched *The Indicator*, we made it clear that while we were strongly pro-human rights, anti-apartheid and broadly supportive of extra-parliamentary groups, we would be non-partisan in our ideological approach. Initially, we were under strong pressure to take sides in the extra-parliamentary battle, but we resisted. We focused on human rights. *The Indicator* is the only newspaper in South Africa that gives a human rights award, and which has announced that human rights and civil liberties activities would largely determine our coverage.

I should like to believe that after initial skepticism, all the groups have come to respect *The Indicator*'s independent stance. This is reflected in the range of articles submitted to us by people right across the ideological spectrum. I should also like to believe that we have earned a reputation for integrity, for *The Indicator* is one of the very few newspapers to have access to leaders in all rival anti-apartheid groups. We even get government ministers to talk to us when they take time off from threatening us.

We are fortunate too to have good relations with many mainstream newspapers. Most of them use our articles, though one or two have, without admitting it, decided that we are too radical and can't be trusted. The irony is that when we submit the same articles to the South African Press Association, they go to the newspapers without our byline, and then those articles are used in those same papers.

The Indicator also submits articles to a wide range of newspapers, magazines and TV and radio stations, mainly in the United States and Western Europe, though we lack the resources to maintain a consistent supply. Just to give you an idea, until late 1988 we had a staff of four full-time people putting out an average of 72 pages a month. Those four people had to deal with editorial, advertising, make-up, production, accounting, the whole lot. We are now up to seven people, but it has meant working sometimes up to 17 hours a day consistently. We have a very dedicated staff. I don't think that we are going to be able to last at that pace much longer. We also monitor the major newspapers in South Africa and are involved in a continuous battle to get them to publish articles that would give a better balance.

Earlier I mentioned that we had often thought about throwing in the towel. So long as we are able, we won't give up. Perhaps my attitude is racist, but I will need something extraordinary to lure me back to work for a white newspaper, grateful as I am to *The Rand Daily Mail* for having given me a wonderful opportunity to learn about the media under so many great journalists. Far from throwing in the towel, it has become absolutely vital for us in the emerging press to provide training and facilities for black journalists, and in particular and especially for women.

I cannot fathom why, with such huge amounts of money being poured into projects in South Africa from abroad, that *The Indicator's* training project is bypassed. Perhaps because I am not too diplomatic in sugar-coating my words and I speak out of turn and am a little too abrasive. But I suppose that is now the yardstick against which we are measured.

Recently an American church group agreed to give us a small grant if we trained and employed at least one black woman journalist. *The Sowetan* newspaper published a little article in which candidates were asked to apply. The result was that we had some 250 applications. Many were chancers, but some were from gainfully employed honors graduates who said they were prepared to take big salary cuts simply to be given the opportunity to do something they have always wanted to. The problem is, we can't afford to give the chance to even a handful whom we regard as potentially good journalism prospects.

This constant search for assistance takes up a considerable chunk of our time. Fortunately for us, the Canadian government has now also promised us a small initial grant, certainly not adequate for our purposes, but extremely welcome all the same, which will enable us to train and employ two more people, one in production and one in editorial.

If this sounds like a commercial for training grants, I make no apologies. The future of South African journalism is already under the cloud of government action, but equally it cannot survive without trained, professional journalists. In the present set-up, and even in the inevitable new society, independent professional journalists will continue to play a crucial role. And if this conference does nothing more than take heed of our plea for assistance in helping to counter the conspiracy of deception and at the same time help train more young people, then I will deem it a success and well worth having made the trip for.

The government cracks down on South Africa's first anti-apartheid newspaper published in Afrikaans.

"We're more subversive in their eyes than anybody else, because we come from where they come from."

By Max du Preez

The National Party, which has ruled South Africa since 1948, has been the vehicle for Afrikaner nationalism. It has been the policy of the government to keep its own people uninformed and in the dark. It's been a conspiracy of providing no information to the ordinary people. The whole approach has been one of "trust your leaders", in an Old Testament sense. A lot of us in Afrikaans journalism have been unhappy about this, but our only alternative has been to go to English-language newspapers. Personally, I felt the resentment at not being able to practise my profession in my own language. I think Canadians will understand how important a person's language can be to him.

After we went to Dakar in 1987 to talk to the African National Congress, we started getting feedback from the newspapers back home, and it was incredibly negative. We were called traitors, and when we arrived back at the airport in Johannesburg, we had to be escorted by police and go home one by one. I was told this would continue until we put out a newspaper in Afrikaans, which we did on the fourth of November 1988.

People at this conference have been talking about the alternative press in South Africa. In my case that means starting a business concern from nothing, no sponsorship, no support from the private sector and with a very unpopular message and with an insecure future. We started off with a 10,000 rand overdraft at the bank and

Max du Preez is editor of *Vrye Weekblad,* South Africa's first anti-apartheid Afrikaans-language newspaper. Du Preez has worked for *Die Burger and Beeld.* He has been parliamentary and Namibian correspondent for the *Nasionale Pers* newspaper chain. He was part of a group of Afrikaans academics who met with the African National Congress in Dakar in 1987.

nothing else. Some of the reporters worked for free and sold some of their property to start the paper. Our future is very insecure because we get no support from the private sector.

What we have in mind is to work towards national reconciliation in South Africa. There has been the old clash between the two nationalisms in my country, Afrikaans nationalism and African nationalism. I think it is important to start preparing the climate for reconciliation. I think we should forget about Afrikaner nationalism, and forget about ethnicity as a part of our solution. We have to work hard to persuade people that Afrikaners are not a monolithic group, and they could make a valuable contribution in a post-apartheid society.

Joe Thloloe touched on the question of whether we go for a non-racial democracy or not. This struggle is being fought in the black community between the charterists and the black consciousness groups. For my side, we have very little choice but to fight for a non-racial democracy, because otherwise we define ourselves out of any kind of significant role in South Africa's future. We believe that Afrikaners should start playing that role now in terms of fighting apartheid, fighting now for a non-racial society.

I think that the lesson that we want to give to our people is not to do what Ian Smith did in Rhodesia — define yourself out of the majority as a little group, give yourselves special privileges, and give white people a block of seats in a future parliament or special privileges for minority rights. We're very much against that. Our message to our people is that we are Africans as much as anybody else.

My forefathers arrived in the Cape in 1652 from Holland. We're French Huguenots. Three hundred years is a long time. I have no other fatherland. I have no other place to go. My absolute commitment is to South Africa, and I see no difference between myself and "indigenous Africans". I see myself as an indigenous African. I'm not Dutch. I'm not English. I'm not French.

There is nothing wrong with being Afrikaans or a Boer, as we call it down there, and also fighting apartheid. In fact, I find it quite a natural thing. The Afrikaner throughout history has always been a bit of a rebel; he always looked for a cause. And I think it's very appropriate for the Afrikaner to now discover what his new cause should be.

Starting our newspaper has been in many ways an unpleasant experience. The reaction of the state has been harsh. We were charged 50,000 rand as a deposit for registration. The normal fee is 10 rand. It's the highest amount any newspaper has ever been forced to pay in South Africa. Two weeks after we appeared in the streets, we got a warning from the Minister of Justice in terms of the *Internal Security Act.* Now that's the short way of doing things. The long way is what they did to *The Weekly Mail* and other papers — the long series of warnings. But there is a short way. They used it last in l977. They tell you, "You're not going to be on the streets tomorrow."

In the short period that we have been publishing, we've been creeping into the hearts of small but important groups of Afrikaans speakers. The National Party has always been very dependent on its intellectuals, on its philosophers. The Afrikaners were largely an illiterate group at the turn of the century, after the Anglo-Boer War. They were an impoverished, uneducated group of people. Our first people went to universities in the l920s, and up to the generation of my father, it was the rare exception for an Afrikaans person to have a university degree. It's now changed quite a lot, but this whole obsession with intellectuals, with academic qualifications, is still there. What has happened over the last decade or so is that these intellectuals have abandoned the National Party for various reasons.

These are our main targets for the moment. This is the call of our leadership, which is small at the moment, but growing. And we have made it very uncomfortable for the government, because these guys, these people are very important to them. They've lost their intellectual backbone completely. We are writing in their own language. So we have hurt the government quite a lot. We are more subversive in their eyes then anybody else, because we come from where they come from.

A lot of people ask if it isn't weird to have an Afrikaner fighting apartheid. My conversion on the road to Damascus was really when the Cape mouthpiece of the National Party, *Die Burger*, sent me to parliament in 1977 and I sat there listening to one Nationalist after another. Over a period of about six months, I realized that my people have become morally bankrupt and sick and there was nothing to be proud of anymore. I think a lot of young Afrikaners are experiencing the same thing, and there is a trickle which we hope will become quite a stream of young people who are joining the struggle against apartheid.

I think the government's strategy is to bleed us to death. We are being sued by the state president, and this is the first time in South Africa's history, that a newspaper has been sued by a state president for libel. And when I go back home I'm going to be in court for quoting a banned person in terms of the *Internal Security Act.* And there is no room for fines. If I am guilty, I am going to jail.

The government and "white liberals" combine to suppress black journalists, says a senior editor of *The Sowetan.*

"As soon as you become a danger to the newspaper, they find a way of throwing you out."

By Thami Mazwai

Being a journalist in South Africa is an apt theme for this session, but I would have been happier if the title had read, "Hammering the Messenger." That is what press restrictions are about in South Africa. In the last two years, one journalist was killed by a mob near Cape Town, and the other was killed in detention. Since 1977, at least eight journalists have fled the country, and about eight were banned. Five from the foreign press corps have been thrown out of the country. Many others have been refused visas to enter the country.

I have lost count of the number of journalists who have been in detention. At the moment there are two. Brian Sokutu has been in detention now for over two years, while Vuyelwa Mhlawuli recently had a eye removed after being shot in the head by an unknown gunman. A third journalist, Zwelakhe Sisulu, is under severe restrictions and his home has been turned into his prison. These journalists are living testimony of the extent to which the system is prepared to go.

While all journalists of conscience have been hammered, black journalists have been bludgeoned. Even those newspapers serving the black community and others concentrating on the crisis in the country are under siege. *New Nation, The Weekly Mail* and *South*

Thami Mazwai is senior assistant editor of *The Sowetan,* South Africa's largest black daily newspaper. In 1963 he served 18 months in jail for involvement with the Pan African Congress, an anti-apartheid movement. He began his career in journalism in 1969. Citing journalistic ethics, he served 18 months in 1981 for refusing to give evidence against a friend. He was the African representative on the International Journalists Federation executive from 1986 to 1988. Currently, he is at Harvard on a management development program sponsored by the university.

were snatched off the streets for several months. Two others face a similar fate. The government is responsible for 80 per cent of the harassment of black journalists. But the remaining 20 per cent comes from unexpected sources.

At the top of the list you will find the newspaper owners. I am referring to the Argus Company and Times Media Limited. Their devotion to freedom of the press is limited to how far profits can trickle into their coffers. As soon as their profits are threatened, their commitment to press freedom simply evaporates.

Five editors have been fired of late by one of the most "liberal" institutions in the country, Times Media Limited. The three English-language editors were Laurence Gandar, Anthony Heard, and Allister Sparks. While the bosses at Times Media Limited have mentioned business reasons for these dismissals, it is too much of a coincidence that all three editors were involved in confrontations with the government. Anthony Heard had actually defied the government. He published an interview with the ANC. Laurence Gandar had been charged for contravening the *Prisons Act*. And Allister Sparks had running battles with former Justice Minister Jimmy Krueger. The other editors who were fired were Wimpie de Klerk and Harald Pakendorf, who belonged to the Afrikaans establishment. They were thrown out because they dared to challenge the state.

This affects us as journalists in the sense that, if the newspaper owners can fire white editors who step over the line, what chance do you have as a black journalist? You are expendable, and they can always get rid of you. As soon as you become a danger to the newspaper, they find a way of throwing you out.

Black journalists find their reports challenged by their white seniors. Sometimes their reports are edited in such a way that a different message is conveyed. If a news editor is conservative, reports about police brutality are challenged. The journalist is made to feel as if he was lying. On the other hand, if the news editor is progressive or liberal, he will expect your stories to show a particular bias. And this means ignoring all stories which give an opinion. It's very racist, and it means that organizations that espouse Africanist or black consciousness causes will not be used, or will be used next to the funeral notices.

The progressive liberal white journalist has two sets of standards — one for the government, and one for himself. If he suppresses Africanist or black consciousness news, it's okay, but if the government suppresses his, he must scream at the top of his voice.

The black reporter journalist finds himself having to write what his boss is going to be happy with. As a journalist, you are an artist and you are a professional. You don't enjoy doing stories and then finding out that your stories are not used. So you are bound to write those stories which are going to get into the paper. This affects the morale of the black journalists. A lot of them have left these newsrooms in despair, angry and disillusioned, because they refuse to have their minds made up for them. They refuse to believe that a truth is a truth only if it appears in this form. They believe they have the intelligence to be able to know what is a story and what is not a story. And that is a censorship of another form.

Having experienced it over the past four years, I believe this insidious combination of censorship from above and self-censorship has become dangerous to the liberation struggle. The picture that has been painted by many so-called progressive news editors, or progressive journalists, is a picture that has a certain bias. It is a picture that tells a story that in South Africa, blacks support only one particular organization, and that is the ANC. That is not true.

Somebody asked earlier, "Why doesn't the Democratic Party just adopt the Freedom Charter, instead of trying to talk about what should be done in South Africa?" I would say that the Freedom Charter must first be adopted by black South Africa. If people were asked, "Do you want the Freedom Charter or don't you?" I think a lot of people would be shocked by the response of the black community. The ANC is fighting for support in black South Africa, and it is vying with other progressive organizations. One of them is the Pan-Africanist Congress.

My analysis of the situation in South Africa is that support for the ANC and the PAC varies from area to area and from time to time. Anybody who has the guts to put it in black and white — which of the two, the ANC or the PAC, enjoys the support of black South Africa — is telling a unmitigated lie. Nobody at this stage can ever say with certainty which of these two organizations enjoys support in the country. The story you get from some of these newspapers is slanted in this way. I think that it is very dangerous, because it is going to affect our struggle for liberation in the long run.

Another level of misinformation, another form of intellectual harassment of black journalists, is the pleasure that many get when there is the rivalry between our black groups. For example, in 1986 three journalists from my paper, *The Sowetan*, were nearly roasted. They were surrounded by a group of youngsters near Pietersburg and they were supposed to be necklaced. Their only crime was that they belonged to *The Sowetan*, and *The Sowetan* is perceived to be a newspaper supporting the black consciousness and the Africanist traditions. Certain people have taken it upon themselves to say that *The Sowetan* is more BCM and PAC, and therefore it is against the struggle.

The Sowetan has refused to take a narrow view of the liberation struggle. We believe that all liberation groups which represent black people have the right to have their news published. The government has banned the ANC and the PAC. *The Sowetan* is not going to enforce those bans by barring news from either the PAC or the ANC. We are going to report on both, because we know that black South Africa supports these two organizations with all the emotions that can be mustered.

Because *The Sowetan* refused to take sides, we were to be boycotted. This is unfortunate because freedom of the press is indivisible. You cannot talk about freedom of the press at one level and at another level condone abuse of the press by activists of particular organizations.

But the major issue is "hammering the messenger", and this hammering is coming from the government. The best way to illustrate this is to tell you about a recent incident. One morning an elderly man and his wife came to me. They had been woken up at midnight by the police. Their house was searched. The man was slapped. The lady of the house was called names by the young policeman. Two young fellows in the house were detained. These people said, "We can't go to the police and report this because the mouse does not run to the cat to report another cat. We want the police to be exposed. We are prepared to be quoted. A reporter can come and see what they have done to my house."

I assigned a reporter to cover this story. He knocked on so many doors, then we got a telex from the police saying, "We refer you to section so and so of the emergency regulations and even though you don't understand this section, consult with your lawyers." They gave a cock and bull story about the youngsters stirring the police and running into the house and the police were chasing those youngsters at midnight. They expected us to believe that. We decided not to use the story because we'd be forced to publish what the police said, and it would convey a false message to the reader. So we did not publish the story, and that man lost all respect for me and my newspaper and the journalist who had come to his house and made him pose for pictures. He called us cowards. This is what has happened to the media.

On another occasion, one of my journalists saw a confrontation between the police and students in Soweto. The police were just looking for action and decided to provoke the students, and the students answered back, so the police had the excuse they wanted and started shooting tear gas. The students were running all over the place, and some of them ran through windows and were injured. The police wouldn't let them go to the hospital. The students expected that story to appear in *The Sowetan*. After all, they saw a reporter of *The Sowetan* there. But nothing appeared in *The Sowetan*. We had sent a telex to the police and said, "Look, this is what happened and a white journalist saw it and may we please get your response." And we got another fabrication about how the police were stoned and they had to react and AK-47s were found in that school.

Our lawyers made it quite clear: "You publish what you saw, it is an offence. You publish at your peril." So the students were disgusted with their media. *The Sowetan* was there, but *The Sowetan* did not publish. Then an interesting thing happened. The police phoned and said, "We sent you a statement on this and we noticed that you have not used it." We got the message. *The Sowetan* had to use the statement, very briefly, but we were to use what the police said. And the students were furious. *The Sowetan* had become an apologist for the police. This is what the media restrictions are about.

Examples like these show how serious the situation is. The media has been made to censor itself. We must ask ourselves, "Is the Minister going to like the story or is the Minister going to hate this story?" And if you believe that the Minister is not going to like the story, chances are that you are not going to use the story. We are also forced to ask ourselves, "Is the political situation such that this story can be used?" Right now, Botha is fighting with de Klerk for the presidency, so the media at this stage can take a chance and publish some stories while they are fighting. They might not spot us.

That is what we've been reduced to. All we're trying to do is an honest day's job and tell South Africans of the crisis facing their country. This is being made an offence by the powers that be. Being a journalist in South Africa is one long frustrating experience. Those of us who have been to jail know how frustrating it can be, but what gives us strength is that we know that there are people that appreciate the job we're doing.

To run a decent newspaper, you've got to break the law, says a senior editor.

*"It would cost us half a million a day
to be closed down. There aren't many days
that we could lose half a million and survive."*

By Harvey Tyson

My paper is a mainstream, anti-apartheid English-language press. *The Johannesburg Star* is somewhere between the *Toronto Star* and *The Globe and Mail.* It's what many call a commercial newspaper. That is, we like to call ourselves economically, politically and editorially independent.

I foresee difficult times ahead for us. I believe in making a profit as a newspaper. It enhances your independence, but there are limits, and we're going through a hard time right now. I expect that we're getting as many problems from that side of our business as from the authorities.

There are about 100 laws in South Africa dealing with aspects of publishing and three or four layers of emergency regulations dealing with the same thing. In my desk I have a summary which runs to 70 closely typed foolscap pages, and that's a summary. There are so many rules and they contradict each other so much that if you were to take it all literally, you would not produce a newspaper.

But let me tell you about the day-to-day problems of a mainstream newspaper. Let me emphasize that what happens to us is much less than what happens to smaller newspapers who have taken up advocacy positions.

Harvey Tyson is editor-in-chief of *The Star*, South Africa's largest daily newspaper, which is published in Johannesburg. Born in South Africa, he has been a journalist for almost 40 years. He has worked on nine newspapers in South Africa and Britain, and has been correspondent for a dozen other newspapers, periodicals and news agencies in Africa, Europe and America. He is also editor-in-chief of the recently established *Saturday Star* and *Sunday Star*.

We publish seven editions a day, a Saturday paper, a Sunday paper, an international edition and a national edition. And we are turning out the equivalent of four novels before breakfast.

We have a readership of nearly a million a day. I'm talking about readership, not sales. And it is right across the South African spectrum, black, white, brown, rich, poor, Christians, Moslems, Jews, agnostics, ANC, PAC, NP, DP.

We do not support any particular party, but I would think that we are that slightly liberal-moderate thing which deserves and gets quite a lot of condemnation at conferences like this. We are called capitalist lackeys by some. We're called communist tools by the others, and we're in the middle of the road where all the accidents happen.

A particularly difficult day on our newspaper would begin with perhaps three reports being referred to the editor-in-chief or his deputy or the daily editor or the managing editor of *The Star*. The less senior editors have referred these upwards. They would already have dealt with perhaps a dozen articles marked "Editor's Attention," which would have infringed the regulations or the law.

Probably one of these articles would have been reduced to a single paragraph. Others would probably be of the old-fashioned political tub-thumping variety. We're very fond of those rhetorical stories in our newspapers, but if they come from any one of 32 or more restricted organizations, they may not be used. If mainly rhetoric, we would not chance using them. If it had something else in it, we would try and use it.

The daily editor might have taken a report for instance about the ANC leader, Oliver Tambo, a banned person who may not be quoted. What we would have done there would have been, changed the quotes into third person, non-attributable. We would say, "It is thought that in the ANC, these things are being said." It is very hard for the authorities to get you on that. And that's the way that we would do it. But again, we would not be able to carry much of that report if the words could be defined, and there is a very broad definition of incitement to racial hatred or to bringing down the government or promoting an illegal organization. And so those words would have to be excised.

We have many such reports marked "Editor's Attention," because our policy is that journalists should report all newsworthy events as a matter of course even if they are subject to censorship. Only the editors will decide whether or not these can be published. This is because we need to measure and we need to test censorship.

We find that we can get around the restrictions about 85 per cent of the time when we are dealing with news, events, incidents and hard news. But what we cannot get around is the fact that most black political leaders are banned, and their views aren't even available to report. We are unable to reflect the crucial debate that is taking place between black nationalists and white nationalists and the rest.

On a bad morning, those three reports which were referred to the editor-in-chief or his deputy would be discussed with our lawyers. The lawyer's role is not to tell us if the reports infringe regulations — we already know they do — but to assess the risk and how to get around it. The literal regulations we break, I should think, five times a day. And I think that many papers do even without knowing it. It is impossible not to break the regulations if you're trying to run any kind of meaningful newspaper.

Our attitude is that if we have a reasonable case, even if it is only in mitigation or moral justification, we should try to publish. We believe that apart from a melodramatic defiance, which would get us closed down, I should think, instantly, it hardly matters what you publish or do not publish. If the authorities want to get you, they will, and it is quite as simple as that in my mind. Often the authorities do act, usually against advocacy journals or the alternative press.

Ironically, a three-month suspension of a quarterly like *New Era* almost fits their deadline and they will not be too badly hurt by it. They almost chuckled, because the authorities appeared to have not understood what they were doing. But a three-week or even a three-day suspension of a mainstream newspaper or *The Sowetan* would probably kill it.

We were threatened with seizure last year sometime, and we got to court in time and we carried on publishing. I had to do a calculation there and then. I hadn't thought about it before, but we told the court that in those circumstances, it would cost us half a million a day to be closed down. Well, there aren't many days that we could lose half a million and survive.

Another irony is that some of our most agonizing decisions are about whether to publish banned material which we know is safe. We know that the government would not really take strong action over this. For example, just before I left to come here, we had a trade union spokesman, Murphy Moroby, speaking for the UDF on the subject of Winnie Mandela. Now the authorities rather enjoyed this situation and it was easy for everyone to cover it. But in fact, in terms of those regulations, we are forbidden to quote a spokesman of the UDF or the trade union movement, so why should we break the rule just because it suits the government?

One has to think about this for a moment. We published because it was of over-riding public interest, and we did it our way. We didn't say that he was speaking on behalf of the UDF, but said that it was one man speaking. He wasn't entitled to speak on behalf of a restricted movement, and so we simply stayed within the rules.

It's Alice in Wonderland stuff, but that's the way you have to play the game. The same dilemma arises when we are permitted to quote banned citizens. And sometimes you'll hear the ANC, but seldom the PAC, quoted on government-run radio. Why should we also quote them, even if it is news? We believe that by granting information the government manipulates the news. But sometimes other newspapers seek permission and it is granted, and then you suspect the story and wonder whether you should use it or not. We usually refrain from printing any government-permitted ANC or UDF statement on the grounds that the report is neither balanced nor fair.

These are little decisions which must be made in their own context, and on this typical day at the paper you may have three or four editorial executives debating one of these questions: How should we do it? Should we do it? What should we do?

Also on this day, the editor-in-chief would probably receive a polite message from police headquarters. A warrant officer, even a colonel, would then come over to notify him of intent to prosecute on some case or other. The editor would tell the police he has nothing to say and refers the authorities to his legal adviser. That is very routine for all of us, I think.

In fact, it happened to me within four hours of getting ready to fly out of the country on my way here. The alleged crime this time was that we published pictures of hunger strike detainees. That is clearly illegal. You're not allowed to publish pictures of detainees, but we thought we had a loophole. I'll see if we did when I get back.

At the moment, two mainstream newspapers — mine and the *Natal Witness*, appear to be receiving more attention than we think we deserve. The *Natal Witness* is a small independent newspaper in Pietermaritzburg where ongoing violence continues among the UDF and Zulu supporters and others. Trying to report fairly on this tragedy, the *Witness* has incurred no less than 13 threats of prosecution by the state. Six of the cases have fallen away without prosecution, and the editor tells me there's seven in the pipeline and he's hoping that they'll go away. *The Star* has about half a dozen potential prosecutions at the moment. We've also been threatened in parliament by the Minister of Home Affairs.

We're also being sued by the Minister on several cases of libelling him. One of our financial writers was raided at 4:30 in the morning by the security police. We've had a nasty 205, the device used against those who refuse to divulge sources.

But through all of this, it is possible to claim that despite censorship, few newsworthy incidents go unreported. More often our black reporters than our white reporters get in the paper, but they do get in, and they do report. But the news has huge gaps.

One example of censorship is when the ANC produced a bill of rights for a discussion. South Africans were forbidden knowledge of this and its contents because of the source. Because it might show the banned organization in a reasonable light. We did report it, and nothing happened, but you could not actually begin a debate with your readers over this. It would be seen as furthering the aims of a restricted organization. So you cannot even get the debate going at that level.

Another example of restrictions on free speech is that you may not express the view that a coalition government involving the major black political movements might be a good thing. That again is furthering the aims of these organizations. It really is a very strange world. We used to name the specific legal clauses of the emergency regulation on every report that was censored. We would indicate where sentences were taken out. We'd have a big sign in there and would say under which law it had been taken out.

The word self-censorship is a very nasty one and we're very sensitive to it. What we were saying was that it was not self-censorship. It was a conscious government move. Well that's been taken away from us as well, because in the last lot of regulations, they even forbade the use of blank spaces and typographical devices or any means of notifying the readers that a story is censored. Every time there's a new move like that, there is a lull of about a week while everyone sits and thinks.

Well, in this case, after about three days we started to carry the panel on page one, right across the top at first, then across the bottom, sometimes on the side, we'd carry a panel which said, "This edition may be censored or is heavily restricted, but we may not tell you how or where." This loophole which we found in the emergency regulation is used in most newspapers now, and it's losing its effect because it's becoming a routine signal.

However, we had one the other day. My paper said, "This newspaper may have been censored. We are not permitted to . . .," and the next two lines had been dropped out.

Finally, I'd like to deal with four stereotypes of South Africa. The first one is that public support provides the mainstream press with some protection from the authoritarian action, and much less protection to the alternative press. Public support does help, but I'm afraid that support for the free press is waning. The majority of the people, blacks as well as whites, are not that interested in press freedom. They've got other priorities. Most whites don't even want to hear bad news, and most black readers have written off the press to a great degree, and they're indifferent to our problems.

A second stereotype is that the English-speaking people are champions of freedom, and the Afrikaans-speakers are racists. That's demonstrably untrue. Many English-speaking South Africans, including Europeans and Americans living in our country, tend to passively accept or to actively support segregation and exclusive power. An increasing number of Afrikaners are challenging apartheid.

A third stereotype is the perception that the press in South Africa is so compromised or censored as to be a mere screen for authoritarian government — a sort of showcase to allow them to operate. This is probably not so. As several eminent western publishers and editors from many parts of the world told us in Johannesburg at a conference not long ago, there remains an area of robust reporting. Even if we cannot champion the ANC or Marxism or the PAC, or publish what the government decides is subversive propaganda, there is sufficient press freedom left worth fighting for.

A fourth stereotype is that there is a freer press in the so-called Front Line states and in most of Africa. I think the test is tolerance of other people's views. In Zimbabwe, for instance, they would no more tolerate the alternative media than they would tolerate a mainstream newspaper antagonistic to the governing party. Not even Botswana, which is in my view the most democratic country in the sub-continent, will tolerate a press that is actively hostile to the government.

Now, we still have a little bit of that where we are, but there's not much, and it's going. And I don't hold much hope for the press in the next couple of years. I think it's going one way and that's downwards. But it's necessary to encourage the concept of tolerance of opinion, the expression of opinion on a broader front than we do.

What should be done from outside? You've heard the view that public support does have an effect. It's variable, depending on mood and all kinds of things. But getting out of South Africa, withdrawing diplomatic, cultural and economic links simply diminishes the outside influence. If you want to win, you have to play. Anyone can add to the fire, or just watch it burn. It's putting out the fire that requires so much skill, and we're probably all going to see a lot of burning in the next 10 years. It's inevitable.

Nigel Wrench

Patrick Nagle

Max du Preez

Anton Harber

Harvey Tyson

Sat Kumar

Pollyanna Hardwicke-Brown, Darren Oleksyn, Ardita Stephanson, Students
of the School of Journalism and Communications, University of Regina

Phillip Van Niekerk

Govin Reddy

Sharon Sopher

Joe Thloloe

3

Getting the Story Out

Foreign correspondents have to contend with a hostile South African government, suspicious factions within the black community, and a world audience that doesn't seem too interested unless there's violence and bloodshed.

Anthony Giffard
Professor of Communications,
University of Washington

Patrick Nagle
Africa Corespondent, *Southam News*

Nigel Wrench
Freelance Broadcaster, CBC Correspondent

Govin Reddy
Editor, *Africa South* magazine

Government tries to force bad news about South Africa off the front pages and the TV news.

"Evidently it prefers a reputation of press censorship to having nightly scenes of violence on the world's television screens or news spread across page one of the major newspapers."

By Anthony Giffard

Since the start of the most recent spasm of unrest in South Africa, the government has clamped increasingly stringent censorship on domestic news media, and this has been applied almost as heavily to foreign correspondents. In the case of the domestic media, the aim ostensibly has been to prevent the spread of violence and preserve some semblance of normality in the country. In the case of foreign media, the curbs have been intended to force news of the conflict off the pages of the world's newspapers and, of course, also from its television screens.

The South African government has long had a somewhat uneasy relationship with the foreign press. It would like to be thought of as an upholder of Western democratic values, which includes a free press. They see this as one way of distinguishing South Africa from the one-party states to the north. The government seems to believe also that if people were to get what they call objective coverage of what is going on in the country, they would better understand the country's policies and be more sympathetic towards them.

As a result, South Africa has accepted a very large contingent of foreign correspondents. At the height of the crisis there were approximately 170 accredited foreign correspondents based in

C. Anthony Giffard is a professor of communications at the University of Washington in Seattle. He is co-author of *The Press Under Apartheid: Censorship and Repression in South Africa,* along with William Hachten. Born in South Africa, he worked as a reporter and sub-editor at the *Friend* newspapers in South Africa, and the South African Broadcasting Corporation. He was also director of the Department of Journalism at Rhodes University in Grahamstown, South Africa.

South Africa, which is far more than anywhere else in Africa. In addition, scores of journalists in South Africa acted as stringers for overseas media.

South Africa makes communication facilities available to correspondents, including a satellite uplink for television. And yet, faced with the current crisis, the government has clamped down on the media. Evidently it prefers a reputation for press censorship to having nightly scenes of violence on the world's television screens or news spread across page one of the major newspapers.

I want to briefly sketch the way in which foreign correspondents have been controlled. I've been working on a study of the effect of censorship on the kind of coverage that's come out of the United States, particularly TV coverage, but to some extent also press coverage. One of my graduate students and I have identified several periods in which different kinds of censorship were being applied. Censorship didn't begin with the crisis of the past few years. There's always been a sort of background level of censorship, a fairly strict censorship. And what's different about the emergency, of course, is the amount of censorship that has been applied at different times.

We've identified several periods, each characterized by a different kind or level of censorship. During the first period that we looked at, which is from about January 1984, there was growing racial unrest when black students boycotted schools to protest apartheid. These protests escalated in August of '84 when white voters went to the polls to vote for a new constitution that set up a bicameral legislature, but excluded the country's majority black population. There was more rioting after a strike by black mine workers, and still more unrest when the troubles spread to Cape Town in February '85 after rumors that the government was going to move people out of the Crossroads township. And then in July of '85, after 500 people had died in racial violence of one kind or another, the government declared a state of emergency. This was a partial state of emergency. It applied only in about 36 black, or mainly black towns and cities around the country.

Among other things, the state of emergency provided for press censorship. For example, one section said that the police could prevent publication of any information or comment about the emergency as such. The regulations were not applied very strictly at first. They were on the books but they weren't actually applied, but the media were forbidden, for example, to identify the hundreds of people who were detained by the security forces, nor were they permitted to enter areas that were ruled off limits by the police. But foreign correspondents could still continue to move fairly freely about South Africa, filing reports without restrictions, that is, in those areas outside of the emergency decree. Nevertheless, they started taking action against foreign correspondents.

For example, in September of '85, the government expelled the bureau chief for *Newsweek,* Ray Wilkinson, because it objected to a cover story about South Africa in Newsweek, and the Minister of Home Affairs, Stoffel Botha, said that the image of South Africa created by the media abroad was distorted. As a result, he said, an emotional campaign was started against South Africa, resulting in sanctions against the country. So here we have a case of the media being blamed for the outcry abroad as a result of the repressive measures that were taken.

The next period of censorship came in November of '85. This was the first big crackdown, because the government banned televising, photographs, recording, even drawings of unrest in any area affected by the emergency decree. And this ban applied to any kind of disturbance, riots, strikes, boycotts, attacks on property, attacks on individuals, as well as action taken by the security forces. Interestingly, this ban applied not to print journalists, but to television people, to photographers primarily. Print journalists could still report on the unrest. Radio and TV journalists could give eye-witness accounts of what they'd seen, but they couldn't actually take pictures and show pictures. There was concern that the visual image was having too much impact abroad.

Once again, the government tried to explain why it was doing this, and so you find the Foreign Minister, Pik Botha, saying for example, that the action was taken in response to what he called "vicious and venomous coverage" by foreign TV crews.

After the first state of emergency was implemented, there was a period of relative quiet, partly as a result of the large-scale detentions that took place. There was something of a decline in violent protests, and as a result, during what we call the third period, the government in March 1986 lifted this partial state of emergency that had applied in 36 townships around the country. And at the same time, they lifted the media restrictions. This didn't stop them from criticizing foreign correspondents. They tried to kick out three CBS correspondents, and then permitted them back in after receiving an apology from CBS for the coverage they had provided.

The end of the state of emergency also meant that the press restrictions were lifted and that TV camera crews, and other journalists, were once again free to get into these scenes of unrest. And certainly there was plenty to report on, because in May and June of that year, the rival black factions were battling for control of the squatter camps near Cape Town. But the violence picked up again and on June 12 of 1986, the government declared a new state of emergency, this time not covering only a handful of black townships but for the first time, the whole nation.

The emergency was declared to avert what the prime minister called the threat of huge and violent protests that were planned to coincide with the tenth anniversary of the Soweto uprising of June 1976 that sparked off rioting and caused at least 600 deaths. Once again, the security forces had sweeping powers to make arrests without charge, to conduct searches without warrants, to ban meetings. The power of censorship was once again increased. For example, the government forbade TV, radio or photographic coverage of any violent protest or police action to curb it. And the decree now made it an offense to publish what they called "subversive statements".

A subversive statement was almost anything, including calls for strikes or economic sanctions. It stipulated that all news about the crisis should be channeled through the government's Bureau for Information. They actually set up a bureau that would give the official line and this is what journalists were to report.

Although the new rules stopped short of pre-publication censorship, the broadcasters were subjected to a kind of self-censorship in that they could file reports, but were responsible for the content if they did. This was not only print but television. And the news organizations were obliged to interpret for themselves the rather vaguely worded restrictions on subversive statements, and so they were in fact obliged to weigh the importance of reporting a particular piece of information that might violate the guidelines against the risk that the correspondents might be expelled. Many of the news organizations hired lawyers in South Africa to review stories and tapes before they were transmitted.

The censorship was escalated even further in December of '86. The rationale for this was that there were threats of massive anti-apartheid demonstrations over the Christmas period organized by the United Democratic Front. This was a coalition of political labor and church groups. There was renewal of violence in the townships, and this led to the most severe censorship of the entire period. The regulations which were promulgated in December of 1986 extended the ban on reporting violent unrest, but also now covered non-violent campaigns by the UDF.

The UDF had planned a Christmas Against the Emergency campaign that was to have included things like black consumer boycotts of white-owned stores. The new rules made it illegal to publish statements that encouraged the public to participate in any kind of boycott, to discredit the system of compulsory military service, to oppose any member of the government in his role of maintaining public order, to stay away from work, and to attend a restricted gathering.

All sorts of things were simply put off limits to the media. Nor were the media allowed to publish any reports on security force action or the time, date, place of any restricted gathering. They couldn't give an account of a speech made at a restricted gathering. They could not print or report anything relating to the circumstances, the treatment or even the release of detainees and by now, thousands of people had been picked up. Perhaps more significant, it was the first time the government imposed pre-publication censorship. All copy had to be submitted to a body known as the Inter-departmental Press Liaison Centre, which operated 24 hours a day and was co-ordinated by the Bureau for Information.

Anyone who distributed material before first submitting it for approval was liable to a fine of roughly $9,000-$10,000 Canadian, or 10 years in prison. I don't have a single case of a foreign correspondent who was fined or imprisoned. Instead, the government took action against foreign correspondents by refusing them visas, withdrawing their work permits, which meant that they could no longer report, or in some cases, by simply deporting them.

This pre-publication censorship ended in May of that year, partly because the level of violence had declined and the government said that it was no longer necessary. But the ban on filming unrest or security force action remained in effect, and this was continued when the state of emergency was renewed in June of '87, and when it was renewed for a second time in June of 1988. That state of emergency remains in effect now, and so do the curbs on reporting of various kinds.

All of this suggests several questions. One is whether curbs, censorship of conflict situations like this, can in fact force a story off the news. Can it get those reports off page one? Can it get it off the nightly television news? Richard Manning, the *Newsweek* correspondent who was also kicked out, said that TV faces a stern test. He wondered whether it's reached a level of sophistication that will allow it to report consistently from South Africa "without the bang bang", as he put it.

Another question is whether these curbs have changed the kind of news reporting that came out of South Africa. Did it force a different kind of reporting? Did it oblige reporters to go for stories that might be more acceptable to the authorities than had been the case before censorship? I hope others at this conference can help answer these questions.

Government effectively puts the lid on South Africa discontent.

"The townships are quiet because of the overwhelming presence of police and soldiers, not because American network viewers have been denied their nightly fix of burning tires and stone throwing adolescents."

By Patrick Nagle

I am a foreign correspondent, a Canadian journalist of more than 30 years experience, almost all of it in print — metropolitan dailies, major magazines and agencies. My job has always been to get the story out, not to get involved in the story. The professional code of conduct I was educated under calls for the clinical separation of personal opinion from the topic being reported.

It is still a basic tenet of print journalism to keep the reporter out of the story. And I still find it difficult to stand up at a symposium like this and become a part of the story, not an observer of it. That said, I can also say that no Canadian of my age and background would fail to be repulsed by the current South African situation.

As Africa correspondent for the Southams for almost four years, I consider it an essential responsibility to maintain the hard-won access we have to South Africa. This was earned during almost 15 years of continuous bureau operation on the continent, the longest-standing Canadian news coverage of Africa. At times, this means conforming to the press control regulations under the South African state of national emergency. These censorship laws are arbitrary, capricious and degrading. Failure to comply can mean the loss of the essential South African work permit and consequent deportation.

Patrick Nagle was African correspondent for Southam News of Canada for four years. The winner of many awards, he has reported from every continent except Australia. He began his newspaper career in 1956 on the sports and rewrite desk of *British United Press* in Montreal. He has worked for the *Vancouver Sun*, the *Montreal Gazette*, and *Weekend Magazine* and has covered the wars in Vietnam and Bangladesh. In 1984 he joined Southam News in Ottawa. A year later he went to Harare to take over Southam's African bureau. He became Halifax bureau chief for Southam news in 1989.

Since the current state of emergency was declared in July '86, more than 250 foreign journalists have either been refused visas, have not had their visas renewed, or have been deported by the South African government. I would be less than honest with you if I did not say that I find this situation intimidating — that is the plain intention of South African press law. They have not yet resorted to the direct censorship of foreign correspondents' copy. Rather they issue a vague set of directives, which can be enforced on the spot by any police officer who says he believes a reporter has transgressed the regulations.

Virtually all my assignments in South Africa have been carried out in state of emergency conditions. The exclusion of international television reporting has been the most significant aspect of this period. Local television is totally controlled by the government. And more than 20 million people in South Africa do not have electricity in the home, so that a television is an extraneous influence on the black population so far.

Foreign print journalists are not at present confined as stringently as are the domestic newspapers. To be a South African journalist working in South Africa these days is a very courageous thing to do. They carry a much bigger load of controls and have to live with a much higher level of threat and harassment than does a foreigner.

All this has a bearing on the subject of the panel: the problems of getting the story out. This is not a problem. The story is out. There are only three things you need to know about South Africa to understand what is happening there, and they are all in the public domain:

1. There are approximately 25 million blacks and five million whites in South Africa today.

2. Not one of those blacks has any say in the national government of South Africa.

3. This situation is maintained by force of arms.

Those three facts, which are not difficult to grasp and remember, have governed the ebb and flow of the South Africa story for the past 40 years, and they have been public knowledge for at least that long. The Pretoria government does not deny these facts. It does not censor them. That is the real story. That is what animates South African life today. All the violence, all the brutality, all the misery and the fear that poisons the country stems from that source. Naturally, over the years, there have been numerous variations and intellectual glosses that surround that story, but that's 40 years of turmoil.

White supremacy was entrenched in the perverted judicial system known as apartheid, the doctrine of separate cultures. The apartheid system is now crumbling under the weight of its own inane enforcement. And any committed South African will tell you the issue is not apartheid anyway. The issue is power — political power, economic power and cultural power. This story is not reaching its intended audience. Since I've lived in Africa, I do not know the reasons why otherwise-sane North Americans and Europeans will continue to ask, "What is all the fuss about? Why can't the black South Africans settle down and enjoy the fruits of a wealthy economy? Why must there be continuing strife in streets and townships?"

I don't think a person has to live in Africa to recognize how patronizing, how offensive, how racist such an attitude is in the face of the elementary three facts I enumerated earlier. There is a revolution going on in South Africa and it is not pretty. It is not organized into orderly compartments. In the absence of legitimate political structures for black South Africans, the vacuum is filled by people fighting for turf. Although this situation is entirely the creation of the white South African government, they have turned it to their propaganda advantage abroad by the police designation, black-on-black violence. Such a phrase is both tendentious and misleading. A Mafia shoot-out is not white-on-white violence; it is a failure of the civilized order.

That is what is happening in South Africa. Order is failing because huge numbers of legitimate citizens have no standing in the order.

Getting that story out has not been difficult. There are still the clouds of tear gas. The dog squad charges still go on. These are just the outward manifestations of what is happening. Getting people to understand the story has been a far greater problem. The South African claim that banning television cameras from the townships has restored order is just plain laughable. What order there is in the townships is a sullen compliance with their occupation. The townships are quiet because of the overwhelming presence of police and soldiers, not because American network viewers have been denied their nightly fix of burning tires and stone throwing adolescents.

My point is that the press's role in getting the story out is a minor one if Canadians can't identify this as the biggest single abuse of human rights since World War II. It's difficult for me to understand why we have to keep explaining this, but it goes on. I like to use the example of the Commonwealth Eminent Persons Group and their mission to South Africa. These people were not just interested bystanders. They were not stupid. They were not uninformed. Nevertheless, they had to begin their mission report with a sentence that was desolating to all of us who covered South Africa during the period, leading up to and during their study: "None of us was prepared for the full reality of apartheid."

They saw nothing that had not been seen before. They did nothing that had not been done before, yet they were unprepared for what they found.

The story of South Africa is out there for anyone to see, but few seem prepared to accept such direct evidence. The South Africans have been extraordinarily successful in blaming the press for their woes. They have nothing more to fear from the press. The story is out, and nobody is doing very much about it. Racial, economic and political segregation still govern the lives of all but a handful of South African blacks. That story is not going to change soon, even if the current palace uprising against P.W. Botha is successful. But really, no one should ever be as surprised as were the Commonwealth Eminent Persons ever again. The potential for chaotic and violent change in South Africa has never been greater, and that story is out in the open too. What the world does with this information would have to be the subject of another conference.

Government sees foreign correspondents as 'villains and thieves'.

"The authorities create an intellectual environment. Actually it's an anti-intellectual environment, one that discourages thinking and inquiry. It's censorship of the mind. Foreign correspondents entering with fresh thoughts and fresh views on this landscape are not welcomed."

By Nigel Wrench

At the annual Foreign Correspondents Association banquet in Johannesburg in 1988, the Foreign Minister, Pik Botha, for some reason only known to the Foreign Association, had been invited as the guest of honor. The Foreign Minister lost his temper. That's not unusual. What was unusual and revealing was the extent to which he lost his temper. By the end of the evening, after an hours questions, which he fought off tenaciously, he addressed his audience, quoting a celebrated Afrikaner president, as saying, "Ladies and gentlemen, friends, villains and thieves."

There was no doubt which category foreign correspondents were in, and Pik Botha strode off into the night, refusing even a vote of thanks from the usually mild-mannered BBC Radio correspondent. Botha spent the evening making remarks like, "I know the black man. I've lived with him, and he doesn't want majority rule." He said things like, "You don't know Africa." His answer to my question about the fate of *The Weekly Mail,* which had just been suspended from publication by the government, led the editors to launch a law suit against him the next morning. It was that sort of evening.

Nigel Wrench was born in England but has spent most of his life in South Africa. His journalism career began in radio, working at an independent station. He has reported from South Africa for CBC Radio News and Sunday Morning, as well the Australian Broadcasting Corporation, Independent Radio News and National Public Radio. In 1989 he left South Africa. He has since been in England and traveling around the United States and Canada.

But what it illustrated vividly, perhaps more vividly than ever before, was the government's contempt for foreign correspondents. No one ever retracted any of Mr. Botha words. They remain. Neither he nor his staff apologized. Pic Botha that night may have lost his temper. Maybe he had one too many drinks, but he was simply and starkly laying out the ground rules.

In South Africa, as a foreign correspondent, you either accept the government's view of things — as in, "We know the black man and you don't know Africa" — or as a foreign correspondent, you don't accept the government's view of things, and you risk the wrath of the authorities. What the government wants is for journalists to report its version of reality — the "apartheid is no more" version.

Quite frequently on state television, there are pieces about a place called Khayelitsha, which is near Cape Town in the south of the country. The government's version of this reality is that it's a model black suburb. On TV you see neat rows of pastel-colored houses with shiny black faces peering out of pastel-colored front doors. Now for all I know, those houses, front doors and faces actually exist. The government is constantly urging foreign correspondents to report on them. But the broad reality of this Khayelitsha is quite different. Actually Khayelitsha is a wind-swept sprawling state-created settlement on sand dunes about 20 miles from Cape Town. It's the only place in the area where blacks were allowed to live. There's 80 per cent unemployment there. For the 200,000 who live there, home isn't a pastel-colored house but a corrugated iron shack or perhaps a plastic shelter with a number on it somewhere to show that it's government-approved.

A TV colleague recently took the government at its word and she visited and reported on Khayelitsha, as the government is constantly urging foreign correspondents to do. She found the sand dunes and the squalor, not the one street of shiny faces and pastel-colored front doors, and that was her story. The government instantly complained when the story aired on TV in London. "This wasn't true," they said. Of course it was true. It simply didn't align with the government's version of reality.

People like Pik Botha may actually believe the TV pictures of Khayelitsha. Certainly he's never been there. After all, these TV pictures are beguiling evidence that apartheid produces model towns. The truth is that it doesn't, and that is what the government doesn't want others to hear. So the authorities create an intellectual environment. Actually it's an anti-intellectual environment, one that discourages thinking and inquiry. It's censorship of the mind. Foreign correspondents entering with fresh thoughts and fresh views on this landscape are not welcomed.

It's as if South Africa is voluntarily becoming another Albania, applying internal intellectual sanctions and putting up barriers against the world beyond its borders. So when you're trying to get the story out, that's the environment you're in — one that defines your very presence in South Africa as hostile, negative and damaging. I suppose that environment is the most subtle of its weapons. It's the environment that you arrive in if you're a foreign correspondent like Patrick Nagle coming into South Africa. In my case it's the environment you grow up in. It's not one that encourages you to do all those things you need to do when you're a foreign correspondent — to think and to enquire.

Let's take a small example. A while back, there was a protest march in central Johannesburg. It wasn't a terribly big one. The marchers spilled out of a meeting, and chanting slogans and, waving the odd banner, they marched uptown. It was a little march, about 50 or 100 people. And along with a clump of other foreign and local journalists, I followed the marchers, who reached the railway station before the police came. Now this is where the march, in conventional news values, might just become a story. Until this point, it would be little more certainly than a punctuation mark in any CBC newscast, for example. It certainly wouldn't make any of the major morning or evening bulletins, but if the police took action against the marchers, that would be another matter.

But the trouble was that journalists aren't allowed to be at the scene of any police action or anything that they define as unrest. So on this Johannesburg street that summer's afternoon, while the police put on their gas masks, reporters could either leave, as the law requires, or stay and risk arrest. I put my tape recorder in a carrier bag and tried to look like a bystander, not a journalist, just to make my presence legal. Of course, the television camera crews simply left. There was no point, they argued, in their being there when you couldn't take pictures of the news event.

If you did comply with the law and leave, you'd have to rely on the police for what happened next. If you didn't, you might risk arrest. On that occasion, the police didn't arrest any reporters. They fired some tear gas, which you could report in the passive voice, not mentioning the police. So my report said something like, "Tear gas was fired at the protesters", omitting the fact that the police fired the tear gas and that I was at the scene. This way at least you could hint at what happened. So you skate on as thin ice as possible. Sometimes that doesn't work, or you don't get the opportunity to do that. The police might exercise forcible censorship. They might arrest you on the story.

Now the foreign correspondent is a fairly vulnerable beast, particularly in my own case, since we almost always work alone. So if I was arrested, the story simply would not get on to the CBC or on to my other radio stations. Shouting "Deadline!" at a group of armed policemen who believe they can do what they like to you because you're a thief and a villain simply doesn't work.

One afternoon, I heard about a car bomb blast outside the magistrates' court in Johannesburg. In fact, I heard it on my car radio while I was out shopping. Of course I drove straight over. The police had already put up barriers on the roads around the court. You could see the remains of the car. It was obviously a powerful bomb and a big story. But I needed a better look at what had happened before I filed. I spotted some photographers and TV people on an apartment block just across the road. I went up to the roof to join them. You could see the entire scene from up there. But the trouble was, the riot police had seen us taking it all in. They came up to the roof, arrested the lot of us, about a dozen, and took us off to police headquarters. As we waited under guard to learn our fate, my morning deadline for CBC went by. London had already beeped me twice and of course I couldn't get to a phone. For all they knew, I was still out shopping.

Eventually, the police decided to interrogate us individually and they assembled teams of two policemen for each journalist. It turned out they believed we'd been tipped off by the guerrillas that the attack would take place. The bombers had advised us to be on that apartment block for the best view. They listened through all my tapes for sound of the explosion. Of course, what they got was an old interview with a white right-wing leader and the sound of some ambulance sirens which I'd recorded on the way to the magistrates' court. As darkness fell, I was retracing my steps of that day with these two policemen. They couldn't believe that a foreign correspondent could hear about a bomb blast on a car radio. By the time they eventually let me go, the real event, in terms of ordinary news values, the bomb blast in which three of four people had been killed, was just about old news.

London wasn't interested, except for one or two lines of the story. CBC took something under some pressure from me as I recall, but for the most part this forcible censorship, the simple taking of the reporter off the story, worked remarkably well. No reporter, no news.

Under these conditions, it's a very beguiling option just to stay in the office next to the phone, the wire machine and the radio, waiting for the call from the police to let you know what happened. That way you get the story, you make your deadline and neither the police nor your foreign editor ever shouts at you. It's exactly where the authorities want you. It might be, for all I know, where your foreign editor wants you. At least he doesn't have to beep you and think you're out shopping. It's a dangerous option that lures you when you're a little tired of the daily battle. I think that it is better to get arrested on the story and miss the deadline than not be there at all.

After that last example, you might think the actions of the police are a little paranoid, and you'd be absolutely right. South Africa is a place where conspiracy theories are the order of the day. Faced with a foreign correspondent, a policeman simply believes that he must be hiding something. Once after my tape recorder was somehow mistaken for a camera outside Pretoria Central Prison — pictures of prisons are illegal in South Africa — the CID came over and searched my car. They found some music tapes and spent the rest of the morning listening to the "Talking Heads", convinced that there was some subversive material there.

Forcible censorship can take another route. A favorite with foreign correspondents is the threat to withdraw a work permit, and more frequently, to refuse to issue it in the first place. CBC, for example, has never been able to get a staff correspondent into South Africa, despite repeated trying. Or there's the delay tactic to convince a reporter that to work in South Africa is a privilege not a right. I'm a naturalized South African by virtue of having lived there for so long. So I'm lucky. None of this directly applies to me. It's more difficult to throw me out.

But among TV correspondents who do work under this constant threat, there's talk sometimes at cocktail parties or at Correspondents Association banquets, of the work permit piece, the innocuous story designed to convince the authorities that you should stay there — the story that for once you will accept the official view, just to stay in South Africa. It means, as far as I'm concerned, the government censorship tactics have worked only too well. In 1988, Pretoria planned to start a register of journalists for people like myself —

free-lancers and stringers who don't need a work permit. The obvious threat is that once registered, you could simply be struck off and denied the right to work. The aim again is self-censorship, the encouragement of the work permit story and the nice story about pastel-colored housing in Khayelitsha.

After a lot of pressure, the register was shelved, but it's still a very real threat, I think, and one that if implemented would have serious consequences on reporting from South Africa. That's because foreign news organizations like the CBC and Reuters, have more and more come to rely on journalists who are also South African citizens, simply because news organizations can't get work permits to send out staff reporters. The government has seen what they're up to, and is seeking ways to rein these people in.

Forcible censorship can also mean physical violence. Police, believing their power on the ground to be more or less absolute, have been known to pick out anyone who's obviously a reporter. There's TV footage from '84, '85, which shows a riot policeman taking aim at the camera with a tear gas gun and the camera bucks as the tear gas canister hits the cameraman in the shin. It opened a gaping flesh wound. I don't think that the police have necessarily become more sophisticated.

In 1988, I was covering a protest in Namibia, where South Africa's state of emergency and its media regulations do not apply. Protesters marched on the offices of the South African Administrator General in Windhoek, demanding independence. At the heavily guarded gates, I was recording their chants when the police arrived. Since there's no state of emergency, I could technically stay during this police action. But one of the riot police saw my tape recorder and, leaving his colleagues to deal with the crowds with rubber whips, he turned his on me, chasing me down the streets, and striking a few blows over my shoulder. If this had happened in South Africa, technically I wouldn't have been able to report it without official permission, since it would be classified as police action under the state of emergency.

Now there are those who say that these impediments make it simply impossible to report the story at all, and as a protest, foreign correspondents should simply leave. The bureau should close down. Coverage should be pulled back to a front-line state. I think that would simply provide Pretoria on a plate with the ultimate censorship — no reporters at all. It might serve as a protest for a week, an event that might capture some headlines with Western news values being what they are. After that, news editors would simply be yelling for the story from somewhere else and Africa really would become Albania.

I think it's crucial to try, however fruitlessly sometimes, aggressively if necessary. Tony Giffard mentioned a phrase which made me smile ruefully. It reminded me of a time gone by, and not too pleasantly. He mentioned in connection with a *Newsweek* correspondent, the phrase, "bang bang" — "Is there any bang bang today?" And I think that is a reflection of the way the stories too often have been reported by foreign correspondents and I don't exclude myself. The "bang bang", the action, reduces the South African conflict, the horrors of apartheid to skirmishes and to 15-second sound bites.

I remember a photographer at a political funeral, before the emergency, saying, "Okay, we've had the funeral. Let's rock and roll!" He was looking for the front page news magazine picture. He was one of what some have called "the Rambo photographers". And the trouble with reducing the story to "bang bang" is that we're not left with a story at all. Networks heroically promised to keep the story going after the state of emergency, even if it meant a blank screen, they said. Well, that lasted all of a week, and now correspondents, especially from the U.S. television networks, complain of working on any number of stories and not getting them aired. They were trying to get perhaps a new way into the story. The editors wanted the "bang bang". The ratings were calling.

Which brings me back to the Foreign Correspondents Association dinner. I didn't quite finish the story. Not only did the Foreign Minister, Pik Botha, not apologize, but his staff suggested that it would be in order for the Foreign Correspondents Association to apologize for the journalists' behavior. Not only that, but the president of the Foreign Correspondents Association, anxious apparently not to goad the government into withdrawing his work permit, actually did apologize.

That starkly illustrates my final point. I think there is a split in foreign correspondents in South Africa. There are those who believe it's an ordinary story to be treated event by event, "bang bang" by "bang bang", and who believe foreign correspondents should be polite to authority, and there are others who believe it's extraordinary and requires unusual methods. Right now it may not be possible to report, to put back on television screens, those repelling but compelling street battles of a few years back. But that doesn't mean apartheid has gone away. It will always in itself be a compelling story.

I think the task of the foreign correspondent is continually to find new ways to describe the world of apartheid, that peculiar world to outsiders, and if that makes foreign correspondents thieves and villains, well that's too bad.

Zimbabwe a special target of South African disinformation campaign

"Although reporting about Africa generally remains negative and neglected, today the South African machine is more subtle and sophisticated than in earlier days, when its propaganda on Africa was crude and amateurish."

By Govin Reddy

Apartheid is now a regional problem. It is no longer a domestic problem. And that's largely due to South Africa's destabilization activities in the region, which in the last nine years, has caused a total of $35 billion in damage.

The system of apartheid has been built on several foundations. Disinformation is one of them. Disinformation in turn has several strands. One of those strands is presenting black Africa in as negative a light as possible. The distortions and half-truths that the state and state-supporting media have been publishing and broadcasting have been fairly well documented and don't need detailed repetition here. But a few headlines from recent issues of pro-government and establishment newspapers will underscore the point I'm trying to make.

The *Johannesburg Sunday Times* is given to sensational reporting, and is not particularly sympathetic to fundamental change in the country. But it is the country's biggest-selling newspaper, with a circulation of 536,000. I looked at some issues going back to November, and on November 6, the headline read, "Jailed by Zimbabwe because he knows too much", and that referred to a white South African spy held in detention without trial. On February 19, the

Govin Reddy is editor of the magazine *Africa South*. The South African native has a master's degree in African history from Northwestern University in Chicago. In 1987, he was co-ordinator for press and publicity for an international conference on Children, Repression and the Law in South Africa, held in Harare. Reddy spent five months in a South African jail in 1976, after being imprisoned without trial. He was granted political asylum in Zimbabwe in 1981, where he now lives and works.

headline read, "Zimbabwe minister beaten by a white". Now, those were the only two stories on Africa in 16 issues over a period of four months, and both, although true, were negative.

The Citizen newspaper was established by government slush funds in 1977 and survived the information scandal of the time. It is now a so-called independent paper which faithfully mouths National Party policies and it could correctly be described as an English-language mouth piece of the regime. I looked at issues in January and February and on January 12, it had this title: "Zimbabweans starve as food runs out". Now that is not a distortion but an absolute lie, because Zimbabwe in fact has a surplus of maize and has been sending maize to Mozambique. No Zimbabwean is starving. There has been a drought in the southern province and food had to be shipped from Harare to the south and there were some transport problems, but that was the full extent of the starvation story. But those were the headlines: "Zimbabweans starve as food runs out". On January 27, "Zimbabwe can't make up vehicle deficit". On February 9, "Zimbabwe poison".That referred to Harare as the anti-South African propaganda centre — and was written shortly after the last Commonwealth Prime Ministers' Conference there.

Now *The Citizen* is a daily paper and in two months those were the only stories on Africa, all negative, all distorted, all in Zimbabwe. I'll come back to the Zimbabwe point in a moment.

The Department of Information puts out a publication called *Southern Africa Today*. Its November 1988 issue had the following headlines: "ANC doesn't want Mandela released". "Zimbabwe facing brain drain". Now that's a beauty, because we all know brain drain refers to people leaving the country, but here the story referred to people leaving the public sector and going to the private sector. And then for a change, one on Zambia, "Fear of no beer". So from these examples, it's clear that Zimbabwe is a special target. And the reason is quite obvious. As a non-racial society that is working, Zimbabwe poses the greatest threat to the apartheid thesis, that majority rule in Africa inevitably leads to chaos, ethnic conflict, racial strife and economic decline. That some of these phenomena have occurred in Africa cannot be disputed, though the mainstream media rarely refer to causes. In Zimbabwe, apart from a brief period of ethnic conflict which has been amicably settled, none of these things happened after independence and majority rule.

On the contrary, the whites are doing better economically than they did under 15 years of UDI. The agriculture-based economy, despite being hampered by several years of drought, has shown steady growth, and corruption has been tackled by a public commission of inquiry which has already led to the resignation of two cabinet ministers. All this, of course, poses a major challenge to the basic tenets of apartheid. Not surprisingly then, Zimbabwe receives the most negative of an overall negative press on black Africa.

Although reporting about Africa generally remains negative and neglected, today the South African machine is more subtle and sophisticated than in earlier days, when its propaganda on Africa was crude and amateurish. Through radio and television, over which the government has an almost total monopoly, the regime not only exercises an enormous influence on the country's white population, but on a growing number of black listeners and viewers, most of whom do not have access to the alternative press or overseas publications.

Through a variety of publications and the external service of SABC, it also reaches readers and listeners all over the world. Its radio signals in Africa are particularly strong, in contrast with *Radio Freedom.* You try to tune in to *Radio Freedom* and you invariably end up picking up *Radio South Africa*. Pretoria has also set up a radio station specifically to broadcast propaganda to Zimbabwe, again underlying the importance it attaches to that country in the propaganda war. That station is euphemistically called *Radio Truth.* The regime's list of publications include the glossy *Panorama*, focusing on internal issues, and the equally glossy *Southern Africa Today* which focuses both on South Africa and Africa. These magazines reflect a new sophisticated approach to its propaganda. News is presented selectively and partially.

South Africa's acceptance by black African countries is a favorite theme. Almost an entire issue of *South Africa Today* was devoted to Botha's foray into black Africa last year. Black writers write sympathetically about apartheid. A regular column in *Southern Africa Today* is written by Veli Mashumi, whose defence of apartheid has gone so far as to justify the death sentence on the Sharpeville Six.

A letters page contains letters from readers in black Africa, and they write about how enlightened they have become about South Africa thanks to *Southern Africa Today.* Yet another glossy magazine is *Southern African Connection,* a quarterly publication which focuses on business and economics. Purportedly published by an independent company, it bears the unmistakable stamp of the Department of Information. The message this magazine tries to deliver is this: South Africa is the economic powerhouse of the region; therefore, remain on friendly terms with South Africa, which means accepting apartheid, and all the countries of the region will benefit from South Africa's wealth and industrial development.

Because of the state of emergency and the crackdown on the alternative media, the regime's disinformation campaign takes on an even more ominous note. The state media and other media committed to the status quo now operate in much bigger space. As the voices of dissent and resistance slowly disappear, the state moves in to fill the void. If we look at the other side of the same coin, we will see another void, and one that is often neglected or at least is not often noticed. I refer here to the state of the media in the independent South African countries.

The media in these countries is so underdeveloped that one of the major stories of the world, right on its door step, was appallingly covered. Take again the case of Zimbabwe. It is economically SADCC's (Southern African Development Coordination Conference) most developed country. *The Harare Herald* is Southern Africa's second biggest selling daily newspaper, second only to *The Johannesburg Star*. Its coverage of foreign news in general and South Africa in particular is abysmal. Newspapers in Tanzania and Zambia are just as bad. There appear to be several reasons for this.

Firstly, shortage of paper, shortage of ink and equipment. This limits the number of pages that each paper can print on a particular day. *The Herald*, with a circulation of over 150,000, sometimes appears with as little as eight pages. Its average is about 12 to 14 pages. That's much smaller than the Regina newspaper and Harare has a population of about 800,000 and Regina I believe has about 150,000. With so few pages to work with, domestic issues almost always take precedence over foreign news, which is generally limited to a few scanty reports. There are almost no analytical features.

Secondly, there is also a political problem in that most of the media in these countries is either official or semi-official. Hence an inordinate amount of space is given to speeches by heads of state and cabinet ministers, no matter how inane the subject. Radio and TV, wherever TV exists, are also under state control and here, too, domestic issues and protocol news take priority.

The third problem lies with newspaper editors and heads of radio and television stations themselves. They either lack an international perspective or feel their careers are better served by reporting every minister's sneeze. None of these papers has its own correspondent in South Africa and they tend to rely on news agencies like SAPA, the South African Press Association, even when alternative news sources are available, for instance, Inter-press Service, a Third World agency and the alternative news agencies inside South Africa, and there are quite a few of them.

The fourth problem relates to the level of journalism in the region. Southern Africa is remarkably lacking in qualified competent journalists who could go beyond descriptive writing. As a result, local newspapers depend on agencies like Gemini for analytical features on South Africa or even on Southern African issues, which ought to be analyzed by South Africans themselves. An even greater state of affairs prevails in Lesotho, Swaziland and Botswana. For historic, geographic, economic and political reasons, the press in these countries is so underdeveloped that South African newspapers, radio and TV dominate the mass media market.

South African papers like *The Star* and the *Sunday Times* generally out-sell local newspapers in all three countries. Botswana has no TV of its own and gets both SATV and BOP TV. BOP TV is the television station of the Bophuthatswana, which borders on Botswana. The result is that the head of Bophuthatswana is better known among urban Botswanans than their own president. Swaziland and Lesotho have rudimentary TV programs, leaving SATV by far the largest viewership. In looking at strategies and solutions, these countries deserve special attention. Although most South Africans may have a gut hatred of apartheid, their understanding of the dynamics of the South African struggle is shallow, and that is largely attributable to the state of the media in these countries.

I would like to suggest four possible areas for consideration to rectify this situation. The first and obvious one is strengthening or at least ensuring the survival of the alternative press in South Africa. The second one is to strengthen the media in the independent Southern African countries, by especially supporting the few independent papers, and also supporting new initiatives. And thirdly, by establishing regional newspapers, magazines and radio stations to fill the information gap and also to counter the kind of South African propaganda that I outlined here. I'm editing a new regional news magazine called *Africa South*. It hasn't yet been officially launched. It will be officially launched in July or August 1989. The fourth one is training, because we desperately need good competent qualified journalists in the region.

4

Picture Power

Film and television have special power when it comes to telling the story of South Africa. A hundred feet of film from the Sharpeville massacre in 1960 changed the world's perceptions. Now the government has put severe restrictions on what can be photographed, and the story is disappearing from the screen.

Brian McKenna
Documentary Producer

George Hoff
CBC-TV Foreign Editor

Sharon Sopher
Film-maker

Peter Davis
Film-maker

TV is the major field of battle in the censorship war.

"The white rulers so fear the power of the medium that they have taken severe measures to banish the image of rebellion and the terror they utilize to suppress it. They have seen the statistics that the vast majority of our citizenry in the Western world get most of their news from television."

By Brian McKenna

I want to say at the outset, to my regret, that I have never set foot in South Africa. Most of what I have learned about South Africa comes from this conference. But as a documentary producer for television, I've worked extensively in countries where the information issues are dramatically similar to South Africa. I was in Argentina doing a documentary on torturers as the regime was still "disappearing" journalists. I worked in El Salvador as the regime systematically targeted journalists, not with press laws, but with death squads. International journalists, such as the Dutch TV crews so brutally murdered, were attacked as savagely as the local reporters who still, in El Salvador and Guatemala, risk torture, disemboweling and decapitation to do their stories.

Killing reporters is, of course, the most effective form of censorship. It silences them forever and intimidates their colleagues. I pray that the extremism of the South African regime never reaches the scale it came to in Argentina, where at least 56 journalists were kidnapped by death squads, tortured and killed. But if it ever comes to that, I know that many of the reporters in South Africa who now routinely risk their liberty and violence and sometimes death, would be prepared to systematically risk life, not out of bravado, but out of a commitment to a fundamental idea of freedom. I think particularly

Brian McKenna is an independent television producer, director and writer. He is a founding producer of the CBC-TV current affairs show "the Fifth Estate," co-author of a biography of former Montreal Mayor Jean Drapeau, a former parliamentary correspondent. In 1988-89, he was Max Bell Professor of Journalism at the University of Regina.

of the black and white South African reporters who have so illuminated this conference, and also foreign correspondents like Patrick Nagle and Nigel Wrench, whose intelligence and integrity challenge the assumption held in some quarters that a reporter can't hold a heart-felt position and still report incisively, and — dare I use the word — objectively.

The primary field of battle, at least internationally, over censorship by the South African regime, is television. The white rulers so fear the power of the medium that they have taken severe measures to banish the image of rebellion and the terror they utilize to suppress it. They have seen the statistics that the vast majority of our citizenry in the Western world get most of their news from television.

The regime has seen how effectively this policy has worked to their advantage in the present coverage of South African affairs, but I think we might examine whether this is totally true. For example, Professor Giffard's analysis of U.S. network news demonstrates that 80 per cent of the coverage focused on violence, on the infamous "bang bang".

But ironically, by banning coverage of "bang bang" they have forced Western television networks to focus almost by default more heavily on other aspects of the story — not that "bang bang" isn't important. World War II was "bang bang". The war in the Falklands that inadvertently led to democracy in Argentina was "bang bang". The activity of death squads is "bang bang." Yet, too often, the way U.S. television news is constructed, it's often impossible to give context to the violence.

In Canada, the case is different. The news coverage of the most-watched newscast, the CBC *National News*, contrasts sharply with the quick, one-minute, 10-second shots you see on U.S. network news. The fact that coverage is also given some context on programs such as *The Journal*, in intelligent debate and sometimes striking documentaries, further enlarges the coverage of South Africa.

CBC Radio, which has now a world reputation for its coverage of international affairs, has real reason to be proud of the coverage they have given, both on the spot and in sort of systematic coverage of South Africa. Recently even the CBC-TV business show *Venture* focused on the story of sanctions, and specifically on the case of sulphur and other exports. But there should be no self-satisfaction. We're not doing enough, and what we're doing, we could do better.

The fact that foreign editors of three CBC network news and current affairs shows are present here today reflects a commitment that I think will come out of this conference, to do better and to do more. I wish I could say the same about our private networks, whose foreign editors are nowhere to be seen.

CBC-TV wants to return to South Africa but the South African government keeps saying no.

"I would set up a permanent bureau in South Africa tomorrow, given the restrictions, given everything else, if I were given the opportunity. We should continue doing everything we can do. The challenge is to be more creative in getting the story out."

By George Hoff

At CBC Television News, we have not been able to send a correspondent to South Africa since the fall of l985. We had a team, Brian Stewart and Tony Berman, and a camera crew there through the summer of '85 into the fall. We stayed after our visa expired. We sought renewal. It was not granted, and we left the country and have, despite a number of requests for visas, either temporary or permanent, been turned down.

Our problems in covering South Africa really began in the fall of l985. We were in a very difficult situation then. There was lots of "bang bang" and our options were pretty limited. We could use American reports, which we usually did while holding our noses. We felt that we had failed when we aired them. Or we could write the story and we could do voice-overs, using pictures that are available either from agencies or from the American networks. Those were our choices.

As my frustrations grew, I approached a couple of journalists in South Africa. The first one was working for a competitor agency and could not even consider it. The second journalist I approached was Michael Buerk of the BBC. From Michael, I got an immediate "yes",

George Hoff is the foreign editor on *The National*, CBC's nightly TV news program. Hoff has worked as an electronic journalist for 15 years. He has been a producer for CHUM Radio and CTV, an editor and reporter with CBC Radio News, and assignment editor with *The National*. Hoff produced CBC radio coverage of the Los Angeles Olympics in 1984 and the Commonwealth Games in Edinburgh in 1986. He has covered stories in Europe, Asia and Africa, including the Lusaka Commonwealth Conference in 1979. He received an Asian Pacific Foundation grant in 1987.

but I had to talk to his minders, so I called the BBC in London, and got a qualified "yes", which I took as a complete "yes". We found Michael Buerk's material more complete than the American network material. But CBC had little input in assigning him. My phone calls to Michael were more to get a sense of where the story was going, and to let him know how it was playing in Canada, advising him what we were particularly interested in, but I could not assign him directly. After Buerk left South Africa, we continued the arrangement with James Robbins, with less success.

That just gives you some idea of the restrictions placed on us even without the problems of the imposed restrictions that we've heard so much about. There's no question that the measures taken by the government have been very successful in pushing the violence off the screens of televisions in Canada. I would also like to point out that the story has in the past few months reached a plateau. We are trying to tell the story of what is going on in South Africa during this plateau, and with the restrictions, and with the fact that we cannot actually send our own people there — that's a challenge.

Richard Cowan, a producer for CBS, has suggested that the networks seriously consider pulling out of South Africa. He maintains that by staying in South Africa, the American people think that the story is being covered because the networks are there, but in fact, the real story is not being covered. I think it would be a mistake for people to leave because there are enough countries where we cannot get in. I would set up a permanent bureau in South Africa tomorrow, given the restrictions, given everything else, if I were given the opportunity. We should continue doing everything we can. The challenge is to be more creative in getting the story out.

Between September 1988 and the end of February 1989, we carried about 66 reports from or about Southern Africa. I did not include in that the Pope's trip to Southern Africa. Nineteen of the those reports were about the Mandelas, 15 were about white politics, another 15 were apartheid issues, and 12 were Namibia and Angola. Five showed violence or were attempts to report on violence, and eight stories were done in Canada. During that time, The Journal did, I believe, six segments on issues related to Southern Africa. I am unhappy with the stories that were not told, but I think that these figures show we are trying to keep South Africa on page one.

I think that we have to find new ways to tell the stories that are not getting through the self-censorship net and the censorship net. I think it is interesting to note that very few of those 66 stories that I've listed even flirted with the regulations. We have to come up with our own ways around these regulations, and we need to find more ways to get visuals. We need to be willing to break our very rigid news format, to get around the limits imposed by governments.

And while this conference is about getting the real story out of South Africa, at *The National* we have a problem of getting the story out of a whole bunch of countries. In fact, we make more of an effort with respect to South Africa than with many other countries. The latest example is Tibet, where our reporting is extremely limited; and there is a long list of other countries.

We have to be willing to write longer stories, and then report on what we have pieced together, and be willing to make the time to have the anchor read those stories, dare I say it, without pictures. Because we do not have our own person in South Africa, we cannot simply say, "We will do this story and get kicked out if that is the price."

Our next step is that we will attempt to establish a more permanent freelance relationship with a South African correspondent who has access to a television camera and to people who can put together television reports for us. We have undertaken, for the first time since the fall of 1985, to assign a reporter to do a series on Namibia.

These are the beginnings of yet another approach in our reporting. We need to find ways to fit material into a hard-news format, into 22 minutes of daily news, where priority is given to today's news. Recent pictures from South Africa will always have to fight today's pictures from the rest of the world. Since we have no work permits to protect, we should not hesitate, to use more material, but we have to protect the sources in South Africa, and must have some kind of gauge on the accuracy of the material.

I believe Canadians are interested in South Africa and are interested in whatever we can show, even if there is no violence. I recall a story we did in 1985. It was one of Brian Stewart's most effective stories. We had him take us through a working day of a Soweto mother. That was a story that was effective, and it generated as much feedback from the audience as the violent pictures we were showing.

News media should fight back rather than knuckle under to censorship.

"South Africa has literally taken the story off television around the world, taken it out of newspapers around the world, and what has anybody done about it?"

By Sharon Sopher

I don't believe that the press should allow itself to be hostage to any country's press ban. I think that as journalists, who supposedly believe in freedom of the press, it's part of our mandate to fight rather than to submit to any form of censorship that's imposed on us. I don't think that should ever be presented as a legitimate argument as to why no coverage was taking place, because there are ways around that. If the media were ever to use their power to fight censorship, it just wouldn't exist.

There was a closed meeting in which Henry Kissinger participated with about 11 other people, including the president of CBS News, to decide what would be the best policy when the demonstrations broke out on the West Bank. Kissinger actually put forth the argument that they should handle it exactly the way South Africa handled it, and cited how short-lived the world protest to the press ban in South Africa was. The pictures of the West Bank did stop. Many of the same techniques are being used on the West Bank by the Israelis as in South Africa. So I think the danger in allowing a press ban to be successful far exceeds the boundaries of South Africa.

Today I might be covering South Africa. Tomorrow it might be someplace else. I don't want the legacy in South Africa to prevent me from getting the story someplace else. I've travelled a lot, about 200,000 miles, with my film *Witness to Apartheid*. There has been a

Sharon Sopher is the director of *Witness to Apartheid*. The film, which won the Red Ribbon Award at the American Film and Video Festival in 1986, was shot in South Africa late in 1985. It portrays the violence and repression that occurred in the townships, with particular reference to the torture of children. While shooting the film, Sopher and her crew were arrested. She was persuaded to make the film by Bishop Desmond Tutu and Beyers Naude, Secretary-General of the South African Council of Churches.

high level of concern and interest in the issue of Dr. Roberro's death — the black doctor who appears in the film and who was assassinated after *Witness to Apartheid* came out. All questions had to do with my feeling of guilt or responsibility for his death, as opposed to the responsibility of the South African government. South Africa has an Achilles heel, which really hasn't been attacked, which is the fact that it tries to present itself to the world as the last outpost of a white civilization in Africa. They don't attack Western journalists. They attack people in the films of Western journalists.

Because I'm a journalist by nature, if I go into a situation, I know I'm willing to die before I go into it. I would much rather have someone fighting for my rights to be a journalist than my right to continue living as one.

And I think that in the case of Dr. Roberro's death, there's a parallel to the Salman Rushdie incident. And I think there's a lot to be learned from that, and I would really urge you, especially those who are activists, to think about the parallels and what you can do in Canada to go beyond the level of talking to individual journalists about being more responsible. It's the news organizations that they work for and who pay their salaries, that must be confronted.

In terms of the death of Dr. Roberro, what strikes me as strange about the concern expressed is that there were two films in the United States which dealt with the torture issue, mine and one done by a producer at CBS. The CBS film came out a significant period of time after my film, but shared some of the same themes, and someone in that film was also assassinated.

If you draw the conclusion that this kind of film should not be done because people in them are assassinated, you are wrong. That would be like talking to the ANC and saying because armed fighters get killed in armed struggle, you don't carry out armed struggle. I've never heard that argument waged by liberation movements. I think your energies would be much better placed if you looked at what you can do to prevent South Africa from assassinating people who should have the right to voice their opinions. If you take the position that therefore no more films should be done, you're robbing South Africans of their right to speak out. You're robbing me of my right of freedom of the press.

South Africa has literally taken the story off television around the world, taken it out of newspapers around the world, and what has anybody done about it? Max du Preez started an Afrikaans alternative press in South Africa. He explains that when he goes back he will probably face charges of some sort and harassment. I think it's time that journalists form a coalition to stand up to this kind of crap, so that a man who is brave enough to start a paper like that, is protected by his own community.

We have the organs to talk to the world, whether it's print or whether it's television. To use that to protect journalists in South Africa in a cohesive way — that's a power that's just not been tapped. I'm often asked, "Is there a conspiracy not to cover Africa?" I've never met it on a grand scale. What I've encountered has been on a petty level. And that's what I use 80 per cent of my energy fighting. The problem is not how to make a film. I know how to make films. It's finding somebody to do them for. It's coming back with a film like *Witness to Apartheid*, and not having a place to show it.

When people look at the film and have seen an hour of children tortured, what do they talk about? They talk about the Holocaust. At first when that happened, I couldn't understand it. I said, "Where the hell did they get Holocaust from? What jumped in their brain from one thing to another?" Then I sat back and I thought about it and I said, "Well, you know, it's safer to talk about the Holocaust. It is familiar. It's safer because it's over. It's finished. Who's going to ask you to take a stand on that? How controversial could that be?"

But South Africa is happening today, and it's the same situation. It could be time for those in the business to put themselves on the line and say, "I can't go down this path any longer. My news organization should be doing better than this. It should be speaking out." It's much easier to blame me for Dr. Roberro's death than it is to blame the South African government. If you blame me and feel you've blamed the right person, then you can walk away from it and say, "Gee, I feel real good because I know now who to blame for this death."

I found in my experience with this film, after it was finished and I spent two years trying to get it out there, that I had a peculiar willingness to apply a totally different set of standards to South Africa. When the film was finished, I jumped on a plane to England and set up a press conference to get things rolling, came back to New York and the phone rang. It was the BBC, and they said they had contacted the South African embassy in Great Britain to get a response to *Witness to Apartheid*, and instead, what they got was a telegram from Pretoria threatening to kick all of their reporters out of South Africa if they even reported on *Witness to Apartheid*.

It was interesting for me to see how this situation progressed. They didn't back down. They said, "We now want to cover torture of children in South Africa, but we don't know how. Can you help us?" That was on my agenda of what I wanted to accomplish with this film — that it could be used as a tool, to embarrass establishment news people into covering that story. So I said to the BBC, "You don't have to fly over there and make a big production out of it. I can give you phone numbers and you can call, you can talk to people, you can get your story. I will help you."

So that's what they did. They went back. They did three of their own stories. I then went back to England several weekends in a row, to do more press for the film. Then the BBC got Denis Worrall, who was the South African ambassador at the time, on television finally. They'd been trying to get him on, to nail him right around the broadcast time of the film. He finally decided to go on because it was creating a lot of controversy in England. In that interview he made the first public admission that children were being tortured. Worrall was then recalled to South Africa to go before parliament to deny what he said in the interview. He then resigned somewhere down the line.

When the BBC first called me, after they got that cable from Pretoria, their question to me really was a lulu. They said, "But South Africa told us you broke the law to do what you did." I was flabbergasted. I said, "You should be saying congratulations. If this was the Soviet Union, and I had gone there and done an expose on human rights violations in the Soviet Union with a hidden camera in a briefcase, you'd be patting me on the back. Why is it different in South Africa? And how could an honest journalist with 100 and some regulations go out and start reporting and not break something?" Waking up in the morning is probably a violation of some sort if you're a journalist. And they said, "Oh, gee, we didn't think about it like that." If I hadn't responded like that, I don't know what they would have done — maybe trashed the whole story because I broke the law.

Some of the American networks expressed interest in buying my film when they heard about this footage I had. A couple of the networks called and wanted to meet with me. Having worked at a network, I wasn't very impressed with reaching 20 million people. And I wasn't very impressed with being paid money for my footage, because that's not why I went there and did what I did. So what I wanted to know was what they intended to do with this footage and how it was going to air. They refused to discuss it because they wanted editorial control over the footage.

Now I had the film almost finished. I did not want a broadcaster to edit it. I had edited it. "But", they said, "it is one-sided." This was another case of a different set of standards for South Africa. I can't imagine that if I had just come back from Nazi Germany with footage of Jews being burned in ovens, they would tell me to go back and get an interview with Hitler. And I said to them, "You know what my position is. It's that your coverage is one-sided. The only voice you've given up until now is from the government."

I went to Pretoria twice trying to get an interview with anybody in government, because I knew all they could do was cook themselves. I had done another film, similar to this, where the more I talked to the authorities, the deeper they dug their grave. I had never seen an interview with anybody asking the South African government to justify the torture of children. I wanted that answer. They wouldn't let me anywhere near anybody who was an official. They would not do an interview.

So if it appears to be one-sided, that's their problem. What they wanted to do was take this footage and go to the South African ambassador in New York and ask "Do you think these kids were really tortured by the police and soldiers?" And it would come out muddled in some way. And I said, "You're sitting here in New York. I was there. I was there with the people who are going to pay the price for this film. They did not take the risk they took, for you to sit here and play it safe. I can't be part of that." They said that maybe my film would never be seen. And I said, "If it's only seen by three people, but it's seen with the clarity it should be seen with, with the message that it has, then I'm satisfied, and I have done what I owe the people in South Africa who I filmed with."

The film was banned in South Africa. White human rights activists there got involved in it, and it was the most peculiar thing. At the time, when it was nominated for an Academy Award, I knew the South African government would not pass up that opportunity to use that world stage, because it's the largest audience that you can get for anything. They had banned the film as soon as it was nominated. The Oscars were on a Monday. My feeling was that on the Friday before the Oscars, the South African government would come out with some little charade, pretending that it had lifted the press ban on *Witness to Apartheid*.

So I had already met with friends of mine in Hollywood, a black lawyer and a public relations person and people who could help me put together the machinery to respond. I got the *L.A. Times* that Friday morning. Boom, big headline: "Press Ban on *Witness to Apartheid* Lifted". Well, it was simply a flat-out lie. The press ban still has not been lifted. Yet there were people in South Africa, people who were human rights activists, who were applauding the government because they were now going to allow my film to be shown to audiences of under 200 people, which means essentially white theatres, but it couldn't be distributed on video tape or shown to audiences of over 200 people, which means essentially black theatres.

So I said, "This is apartheid film distribution. I cannot condone that. If the very people who risk their lives to be in this film aren't allowed to see it, how can I applaud that as progress, a step forward?" When it comes to censorship, it's like being a little bit pregnant, or a little bit dead. Either you are or you aren't. And there is no such thing as a little bit of censorship. Something is either censored or it's not.

I felt that it was inappropriate for me to participate in anything that would say a little bit of freedom is okay for these people. And when I called certain people in South Africa to get an explanation of why they were giving out these kinds of statements when it was an opportunity to condemn press censorship, I was told, "Well, you can't judge South Africa by the rest of the world. It's different." I said, "You're right. It's so backward that you have a long way to go, but that's why children are dying. And they don't want just a little bit of freedom. They're dying because they want true freedom."

Editors' note:

One of the "certain people" from whom Sharon Sopher sought an explanation was Anton Harber, editor of *The Weekly Mail*, who was present at the conference. His explanation at the conference was that he and others had fought very hard to get the film shown before any audience in South Africa, no matter how small. Thus, what was considered a "victory" by activists in the field was considered a "sellout" by the committed filmmaker.

South Africa's public image largely determined by what people see on TV

"In a world where atrocities compete with each other for time on television, the level of indignation is very hard to sustain with regard to one particular area."

By Peter Davis

I want to endorse what Patrick Nagle said about knowing just about everything that's necessary to know about apartheid. Everything else, everything we talk about now, censorship and so on, are simply nuances. The challenge is for us to transmit what we say, what we know, in such a fashion that somehow, it translates into political action. That is what is meaningful for me, and has always been in my films on South Africa.

I don't make any apologies for this point of view, since I'm independent and I really don't have any master. But in order to be effective, I have to have an outlet, which means access to television basically, because that gives the biggest audience. And it's at that point that problems arise.

Many years ago, when I had been living in the United States for a while, I decided what would be most useful would be to educate the American people about South Africa. And I've also come, over the years, to believe that the American public constitutes, in the struggle for South Africa, a critical mass. I believe that how America behaves with regards to South Africa makes all the difference in the world. I believe the United States has such power — a power which it hasn't begun to exert — that it could, given the will of the American government, rather easily effect change in South Africa in a very short time.

Peter Davis has made over 30 full-length documentaries, many of them award winners, including *Winnie and Nelson Mandela, Generations of Resistance and the White Laager.* He has worked for CBC, BBC, CBS, PBS, Swedish television, West German television, Australian Broadcasting and the United Nations. He has written for several Canadian newspapers and for the National Film Board of Canada. He is currently working on a film on South African censorship and propaganda.

By the time I began to work on South Africa, which is the beginning of the '70s, the Americans were abysmally ignorant about South Africa. South Africa was not an issue. It was enormously difficult — in fact, it proved impossible — to gain access to PBS. In 1974, I had a proposal on South Africa. I went to Washington to speak with someone with the Public Broadcasting Service who was personally responsible for documentaries on PBS. We had a very nice discussion, at the end of which he said to me, "Oh, by the way, where is South Africa?"

That was, as I said, 1974. I didn't get any money at that time. I got money elsewhere. By 1976, I had raised the money. I went to South Africa. I shot half the film, and my crew and I were arrested. The day I left South Africa was the first day I shot Soweto. And I thought that might make a difference with PBS. It took me another year to get that particular film on the air. I also had to endure another kind of censorship. I had to go through a television station. In fact, it was the most enlightened station in the United States. It was WGBH in Boston. I'd seen four pages of criticism of the text that I had written for the film, and I fought about this for three hours in a telephone call. I'd mentioned massacre of blacks in the text, and they asked questions like, "Well, were no whites ever massacred?" I was expected to put in something about whites being massacred. And then as an offshoot of this, "How many deaths constitute a massacre?" And then, just again in passing, I'd used the word "proletariat," and written in the margins was "proletariat, un-American word." After that, I did another couple of films which did not receive any help from PBS.

About 1984 I applied to one of the few sources of funding for documentaries in the United States, for funding on a film on Winnie Mandela. Actually, at that time it was about Nelson Mandela. It got changed later on. I had shot the whole film when it went before this group of peers, supposedly to decide whether I could be funded or not. Everyone was in favor except for one person, a Reagan appointee who was dead set against me. But it had to be unanimous. They passed the funding because this person, whose name I don't know, went out to get a cup of coffee. They passed it while he was away. This was a time when Mandela had slipped from consciousness. I wanted to revive the name of Mandela, and everything hung on a cup of coffee.

So then when working in the United States, you're confronted at least as much by problems related to American internal politics, the workings of American television and the peculiar workings of the American public, as by censorship in South Africa. In a sense, censorship in South Africa has never been a problem for me, because I'm not allowed to go anyway. You just discount it. You either do it or you get somebody else to do it.

Now I want to ask why is it so desperately important for the South African government to gag voices of dissent. The government sees the English-language media, and now even one Afrikaans newspaper, as the enemy, and what is published in those newspapers as part of a warfare campaign that's fought with many kinds of weapons, whose aim is the overthrow of the government under the term "total onslaught." This perception on the part of the South African government is absolutely accurate. Where the government errs is in choosing to believe that this is a conspiracy of all these organs.

In terms of conventional weapons, the enemies of apartheid are extremely weak. I don't believe that apartheid will be overthrown by a revolution as it is popularly understood. South Africa consistently defies cozy historical patterns. It defines itself as it goes along, and that's something that makes it endlessly fascinating. In warfare, victory is achieved when the enemy's will to resist is destroyed. Ultimately this is a matter of morale and psychology, not of tanks and guns.

The government has all the tanks and most of the guns, yet it has not succeeded in crushing the will of the African people to resist. The struggle for South Africa is primarily, at this point, a psychological one, mainly with economic weapons and to some extent, with moral weapons. This is done by undermining the white economy inside South Africa and by weakening confidence in that economy outside South Africa.

South Africa depends on exports and upon investment capital. If markets are denied, the investment capital abroad dries up, and it will go into decline. The point of capitulation will come — if it comes, I'm not certain that it will — when white South Africans realize it is more expensive in treasure, perhaps in blood, to continue apartheid than to dismantle it. You've already seen the fragility of the South African economy in the withdrawal from Angola. For the white South African government to continue, the outside world must be convinced — especially foreign investors — that the country is stable, and will yield a profitable return on investments. For the foreign capitalists, morality does not enter into the question, unless that morality is turned into a force that affects profits.

That is precisely what has happened in the United States in regards to South Africa. When companies like Polaroid and Ford found that business at home was suffering because of their bad image as supporters of apartheid, they pulled back from South Africa. In the struggle for South Africa's future, this word "image" is all important. Image is a public relations word that means how something appears to be, what it looks like to the public. It has little to do with reality. In fact, it's often directly contrary to reality and is intended to distract one's gaze from reality. Those who wish to defend South Africa present it as a country moving towards multi-racial democracy, where human dignity for everyone can be guaranteed if there is no interference from the outside world.

That is the semblance, the image, and the struggle for control of that image is vital to the future of South Africa in ways that are absolutely concrete. Just as in the world of Madison Avenue an image has a cash value, so it does in South Africa. The attempt to impose its image on the world has involved the government of South Africa in a multi-dimensional propaganda and disinformation campaign that's gone on for a quarter of a century.

I want to take you back now to 1960, to an event that left an indelible imprint on the mind of my generation. This was the Sharpeville massacre. I remember the shock of it, because it was the first proof that apartheid was not simply an injustice, but a murderous one. There were reporters at the scene, but no cameramen. Still camera people were there soon after. The film camera people came later to record the gathering up of the bodies.

Now of the actual event of Sharpeville, there's probably about only 100 feet of film, which is two and half minutes. I don't recall whether at that time I saw the news film taken after the massacre, but I've seen it many times since, and use it often in my work. There are bodies of women and men on the ground and a man wounded in the leg sitting up, a women being helped away. What's most striking is the police. Some stand around holding their weapons. Others direct black police in carrying the bodies to waiting vans. None of the white police are helping to carry the black bodies. One policeman, in a special affront to decency considering the occasion, carries a sjambok, a huge leather whip. These were the images that at that moment defined South Africa, defined apartheid to the world.

The pictures were seen all over the world. The result was condemnation by the world community, and the flight of capital from South Africa. It was clear that this was a cause-and-effect situation. I don't know if it has been accurately recorded, when and how the connection between South Africa's image and business confidence came to be understood by the South African government, but certainly by the late '60s, decisions were being made to counteract the negative image of South Africa in people's minds and replace it with a positive one.

A campaign of propaganda and disinformation to win friends and influence people was begun on a vast scale by the Department of Information. They began to produce films which portrayed South Africa as a land of racial harmony, with equal opportunities for all. Other films depicted South Africa as a staunch ally of the West, a bulwark against communism. According to these films, its strategic position straddling the Indian and Atlantic oceans makes it both a guardian of the West or a lifeline from the Persian Gulf, and indispensable for NATO's defence.

All of this propaganda was freely available from South African consulates around the world. For a long period in the United States, which was at that time very backward in the anti-apartheid struggle, this was virtually the only information on South Africa easily accessible to the average American school teacher who, ignorant of the true situation, would present the films to the class. Each time there's a crisis in South Africa, there's a wave of reaction on the outside that has a negative effect on the South African economy. Often international indignation dies down, although repression inside South Africa does not ease. The economy recovers because, with its cheap labor, South Africa can attract foreign investors. This happened after 1960, so that by the end of the decade, South Africa had recovered enough to be experiencing an economic boom.

In 1976 came the Soweto uprising. Now between 1964 and 1976, interest in South Africa had been at a low level. There had been documentaries, yes, but they tended to be tempered in tone. It would perhaps be fair to say that they were conditioned by the appearance of calm, that the whites had everything under control. This feeling was shattered by the Soweto uprising, and a new element came into the picture. What was critical now was that another kind of revolution had also been taking place. The world had experienced a revolution of massive proportions in mass communications. Films shot during the '76 riots could be seen on television in New York, London, Stockholm, Tokyo, the next day.

We saw youths throwing stones and being shot down by the police. We saw municipal buildings in black townships burned, filmed from helicopters. We saw whips and dogs used against unarmed civilians. Almost for the first time, we heard blacks angrily speaking for themselves. And with supreme arrogance, Prime Minister Botha said, "There's no crisis," but the images appearing on daily television throughout the world proved the lie in this pronouncement. In fact, a British documentary took this statement for ironic titling. Once again, after a year of crises and a toll of hundreds of lives, the rioters were contained. But this time, there was a qualitative difference from what had gone on before in the eyes of news editors around the world. South Africa was now a hot spot and newsworthy — a place that could blow up again at any moment.

It was great television. Not only were the riots covered, but news representatives took up residence in South Africa and began to examine what it was in apartheid that drove people to erupt in this way. This was a salutary development. You must remember that from Sharpeville to Soweto, a period of 16 years, there was enough time for a generation outside South Africa to grow up in ignorance of what Sharpeville had meant.

And now I speak to people; I speak to students, and they don't know what Soweto was. What Soweto meant in public relations terms was that South Africa's image had slipped from the control of the white authorities into the hands of the black activists. Well, of course, the black activists were still dependent on white media. Their defiance, their protest, their torture, their dying, defines South Africa, not the game parks, the quaint tribal customs, the economic prosperity and racial harmony that the propaganda films offer.

The propaganda films were now plainly viewed to be lies, and the attempt to present South Africa as a reliable ally of the West was in danger, for no country so predictably unstable could be depended upon. Indeed, if communism was the bogey, then white domestic policies seemed guaranteed to push the black population into the communist camp. And this was not my conclusion, but the conclusion of a Central Intelligence Agency report in 1987. So the South African government itself was furthering the ends of international communism.

There was also a critical change in the image of black South Africans to the outside world. To many people outside South Africa, even many black people, the African population of South Africa had seemed submissive, passive, cowed. The question was often asked, "Why don't the blacks just rise up and revolt?" Then Soweto began to change that image.

Soweto showed clearly that blacks were as willing to die for their freedom as anyone else, that they were not passive victims. This example struck a chord in the hearts of black Americans, who had themselves taken up arms against racism and police repression in the ghetto uprisings in the late '60s in America. Jessie Jackson became an articulate spokesperson for black American concerns about South Africa and Trans-Africa, and Washington faced black organizations that began to lobby. And when the next crisis occurred, which began in 1984, Trans-Africa set in motion the series of sit-ins at the South African embassy in Washington to show solidarity with the people of South Africa. This was the single most important anti-apartheid act that has taken place in the United States. Prominent Americans volunteered to block the embassy and were arrested. At the same time, at American universities there were demonstrations. Typically, students would build a shantytown to represent black living conditions in South Africa in a campaign to force withdrawal of investment in South Africa.

There was a symbiotic relationship with the unrest in South Africa which fed the people who were carrying on the anti-apartheid campaign in the United States and made it easier to get access to the media. As things got worse in South Africa, the government no longer was able to pretend that this did not again constitute a crisis. It declared a state of emergency, which gave additional powers to the authorities. By the time the state of emergency was declared, South Africa had been, for over a year, the focus of attention of the world's journalists, and I think it was something that the white South Africans had trouble with. They had never experienced anything like this before, and they were totally unprepared for it.

I think that's why it took so long for the South African government to take action, especially against foreign journalists. The delay suggested a long debate had taken place inside ruling circles. They had to a certain extent been trapped by their own rhetoric. They had always maintained that they belonged to the so-called Free World, which also meant freedom of the press. This was part of their image. By imposing censorship on the Western news media, they appeared to be cutting themselves off from that noble tradition. The authorities rationalized their move by saying that they were in a situation akin to war, and in wartime, censorship is normal. It was a clear analogy with Northern Ireland and, of course, the British censorship in Northern Ireland actually helps South African censorship.

They also said that the news media actually provoked insurrection, even going so far as to pay young people to commit unlawful acts before a camera. Such charges, which clearly would be a breach of law had they taken place, were never actually brought against foreign news agents and were clearly fabrications. The government needed to convince its own people and foreigners, if possible, that the foreign press consistently publishes lies about the country, and indeed is part of the international communist conspiracy.

The South African government's pre-emptive strike to seize back control of the image of South Africa was amazingly successful. There was some protest from the foreign news media, but they largely capitulated. Why did the Western news media, and in particular the Americans, give in so easily? I think the answer lies in the reason they were there in the first place. The American media were attracted to South Africa not because of its basic injustice, racism, fascism, but because it had broken out into open violence. The inhumanity of the apartheid system, which was there all along, which was first implemented in 1948, had gone relatively uncriticized up until the Sharpeville shootings of 1960. And there had been a decline in the tension up until Soweto in 1976, and then the decline until 1984, when a level of interest was sustained because the violence persisted, until the censorship imposed in 1986 brought about another decline.

American television is only interested in these explosions of violence, its Dracula-life blood. But if its life blood is denied by South African censorship, why are all the television agencies so anxious to remain in South Africa? I'm afraid it's because this drug-like fix of violence has not been totally denied. Bomb attacks by the ANC may be filmed if, in the words of a police official, they show the ANC in a bad light. The strife in the townships which reveals a struggle for power between radical and conservative elements may still be filmed. This has been called "black on black violence." The impact on the viewers is to support claims that blacks are only prevented from tearing each other to pieces by white law and order.

Because of its insatiable addiction to violent images, American television news lays itself open to manipulation by the South African Bureau of Information. The most recent example of such manipulation is the Winnie Mandela affair, which is a public relations windfall for the South African government and will be squeezed for every drop of its propaganda value.

Up until quite recently, I had little faith that sanctions could be effectively applied, but I thought that the struggle for sanctions had great symbolic value and value in gaining solidarity in all the world. Now I believe that the entire anti-apartheid campaign has done enormous damage to the South African government. The economy is in a terrible state, and I think that much of this is attributable to the media blitz on the image of South Africa. Capital, domestic and foreign, has no confidence in the future of South Africa. I think the South African government has come to recognize this as the greatest threat so far to its survival, recognizing the link between the willingness of the American Congress to act against South Africa and the images on television that stirred people to action, that stirred people to move Congress.

The South Africans cut the artery in the flow of images. Under the current restrictions, there is a strong likelihood that if another Sharpeville were to occur, we would have no comparable damning images of it, so it would not endure for 29 years in our consciousness. The government has seized the initiative, and is beginning again to control the image of South Africa. I am pessimistic, but I also want to suggest to you that we have, with regards to South Africa, gone through a period which has resulted in overkill. We've been saturated with images of South Africa, and if we're thinking in political terms, thinking how to move people to action, we have to take into account what the audience is, and how it behaves.

And the audience, especially in the United States, is extremely fickle and apt to lose interest. In a world where atrocities compete with each other for time on television, the level of indignation is very hard to sustain with regard to one particular area of the world. So I think that we should look upon this period now, this enforced period, as a period of regrouping, and be thinking about how we should go on.

5

Influencing the Influential

The South African government conducts an extensive public relations campaign abroad, aimed at persuading people that things really aren't so bad. This chapter exposes the government's propaganda techniques, and offers some suggestions on how to combat them.

William Hachten
Professor of Journalism,
University of Wisconsin

Anthony Giffard
Professor of Communications,
University of Washington

Frances Meli
Editor of *Sechaba*, official organ of the ANC

Angus Gunn
Professor Emeritus,
University of British Columbia

South Africa's uses censorship and propaganda as weapons of political warfare.

"Most of us can see through each of these propaganda themes, but I suspect that there's enough truth in each of them to persuade many who are uninformed or badly informed"

By William Hachten

The government of South Africa has long been engaged in political warfare both with the majority of its own people and with much of the world that has harshly condemned its race relations and the whole system of apartheid. The twin arms of political warfare are censorship and propaganda.

Propaganda is basically persuasive communication that's done with a specific purpose. It's much like advertising and public relations. It can consist of facts, reliable information as well as half-truths, disinformation, deception and lies. Journalism is different than this, in that we are concerned with non-purposive communication. We are gathering information to make available to the public, to use as the public sees fit, and not as government would like that information to be shaped.

I consider censorship to be government restraint on expression, and this is a far more ominous kind of a restraint than any other because government has a monopoly of force in any society, and has the power to jail journalists, shut down newspapers, declare war, do all kinds of things. When we talk about censorship, I do not include editorial discretion. If an editor decides not to use something, he is not exercising censorship, and if the local paper here doesn't carry

William Hachten has been a professor at the School of Journalism and Mass Communication at the University of Wisconsin since 1959. He was a Fulbright Lecturer at the University of Ghana in 1972. He has made five visits to South Africa. He has written five books dealing with journalism in Africa including *The Press and Apartheid: Repression and Propaganda*, co-authored with C. Anthony Giffard.

enough news about South Africa, that's essentially an editorial decision. It's not a censorship problem. It's regrettable, but it's not censorship.

In terms of propaganda, a number of methods have been used over the years by the South African government to counter what South African authorities consider to be hostile, misleading and erroneous information and criticisms that are directed at South Africa, particularly from overseas journalists. And within South Africa, the South African Broadcasting Corporation — both radio and television — has long been a major propaganda tool of the Nationalists and has given all of South Africa its version of reality. They've maintained that monopoly in broadcasting for quite a while, although it is now starting to break up.

I have a feeling that the press tends to underestimate the influence that broadcasting has in the public opinion process, and I think it is something we need to be concerned with. Of course, there are other internal domestic propaganda techniques, weapons of the government over the years, and certainly part of the press. *The Citizen* newspaper has certainly been very much a tool of government after its infamous birth during the early stages of the Muldergate scandal. And also over the years, much of the Afrikaans press has been a tool of the government, although probably less today than in earlier times, due to the increasing independence of the Afrikaans press, especially papers like the *Beeld*, and now of course, Max du Preez' anti-apartheid *Vrye Weekblad*, which is a very significant development in the press situation in South Africa.

To influence the influential overseas — the press as well as the legislators, and the people who make the decisions — the South African government has relied upon various kinds of lobbying efforts, information pamphlets and one-to-one contact, as well as international shortwave radio. The Muldergate scandal provided a marvelous picture of extensive covert and illegal efforts to influence public opinion both in South Africa and abroad, during the late 1970s.

I'd like to say a few words about propaganda in international radio broadcasting. From a huge station outside Johannesburg, *Radio South Africa* sends out a strong shortwave signal and is currently broadcasting about 223 hours weekly. This is up from 183 hours weekly in 1980. That is quite a bit of broadcasting for a small nation. And this includes one hour daily in English to North America, usually in the evenings around 10 o'clock Central Time, two hours in Spanish, one in Portuguese to South America, and for Europe, there are seven hours in English and two hours in French, plus one hour each in Dutch, Afrikaans and German. Two hours daily in English are beamed to the Middle East. But Africa remains RSA's principal target, with seven hours daily in English, four in French, plus one hour each in Swahili, Swana and Afrikaans, and two hours in Portuguese.

There are a few hours at night when RSA's signal cannot be picked up in Africa. I understand it can be picked up in the day time pretty well. And there is good evidence that Africans do listen to it. It often reports news that they cannot get on their own services.

A few years ago there was a major mine strike in Zambia. Zambian media were not reporting anything about the strike but RSA gave very full coverage, an example of how that operates. The propaganda message is subtle and restrained and mixed in with a good deal of hard news and interesting programing. The news, while selective and self-serving, is often accurate and timely. Much of the efforts of RSA should be considered counter-propaganda or efforts to counter the messages of its political adversaries abroad, particularly messages about South Africa.

A recent study of RSA programing found that much of South Africa's counter-propaganda focused on six main themes. I want to discuss these briefly because I think they give you a good idea of the way the people of South Africa are thinking, the way they have honed or refined their propaganda themes. They are particularly concerned with the foreign press, and a lot of these propaganda themes are really intended to answer what the foreign press is saying. And it gives us an idea too of what South Africa would like the rest of the world to think about them.

The first theme, and the one that is most pervasive and is heard the most often, claims that "South Africa is an unusually complex society with a pro-Western government, a vital capitalistic economy, vast natural resources, and a rich cultural life with western Europe." A further aspect of this theme is that "while the nation faces serious continuing problems of race, exclusive focus on this single aspect of South African society by the press and the media of other countries has produced a highly distorted and misleading international image of the nation."

This second point is probably fairly effective, because it is very similar to what many Third World nations had been saying for some years that the Western press tends to focus on the negative aspects of developing countries and does not show the positive aspects. But you can also see that this is another aspect of "hammering the messenger", blaming the media. A majority of *Radio South Africa's* messages, devoted to this general theme, are carried not on the news shows but more indirectly in the cultural programing.

The second theme, and the most prevalent, claims, "South Africa is wantonly and hypocritically singled out as an nation which oppresses its people. The government of South Africa", it says, "is committed to democratic development. To this end, it is working to promote economic advancement, literacy, order and stability, all of which are social preconditions for the maintenance of political liberties. Such apparent abridgements of democracy as they occur should be viewed in that light, and in fact are consonant with the practices of other democratic states", the station argues. This theme was particularly stressed after the January 24, 1988, banning of the 17 opposition groups. Various government leaders have stressed this argument, and then it was picked up in the radio RSA newscast and sent out.

This theme is also tied in with RSA's frequent comparisons of violence in South Africa with that in Northern Ireland, of Israeli soldiers beating Palestinians and reports of uprising and unrest in the Soviet Union. And people who watch SABC-TV have noted that SABC is very quick to show films of racial violence in other countries, particularly if it occurs in the United States or Britain.

A third theme that RSA stresses is, "South Africa has undertaken major programs to improve black/white relations, particularly through increasing black management of the South African economy." This theme often comes out in interviews with business leaders, and I am not sure whether there is evidence to support it.

A fourth theme, one that is harder to accept than any other, is RSA's claim "South Africa maintains a policy of peaceful co-existence and helpfulness towards other nations of Africa." Given South Africa's long, tarnished record of unprovoked military attacks on neighboring countries, and its longtime support of Unita in Angola and Renamo in Mozambique, this seems to be a particularly cynical theme and seems to be one that would be difficult for the government to get across in the face of what's been in the news in recent years.

A fifth theme is, "The efforts to influence South Africa's domestic policies through the impositions of sanctions and divestment are futile and counter-productive." RSA claims that "South Africa's economy is fundamentally sound and its social and political developments are complex, and can be solved best by its own people." This theme, I'm sure, gets a good reception in a number of places where business concerns are paramount, and probably is effective because there are a number of South Africans who are opposed to the government, but still would support that kind of an argument.

In the sixth theme, RSA says, "Political and economic instability is widespread across Southern Africa. The chief sources of such problems are tribalism, incompetence, crime, corruption and most important, foreign interference. South Africa deserves Western support because of its potential as a major stabilizing force on the subcontinent." With this theme, South Africa's propaganda really moves full circle from a defensive position to an offensive stance, and South Africa has really tried to have it both ways in this area. On the one hand, they've argued at times that they are an African nation and you must judge them by those standards. Then, on the other hand, they'll say, "We are a Western nation, a Christian outpost protecting Southern Africa from onslaught of communism, etc."

In any case, the primary purpose of RSA's counter-propaganda seems to be to counter international criticism. And so it's engaged in an ongoing political struggle with journalists and the media of other nations. A cynical, and perhaps accurate, response to these six propaganda themes is to quote the well known maxim that "hypocrisy is the homage that vice pays to virtue." I think it can certainly be applied to these propaganda themes. But beyond that, I think that these propaganda themes also reflect a pretty sophisticated approach to persuasion, and they've come a long way from earlier years. It tells us much about the thinking that's taking place in Pretoria these days.

Most of us can see through each of these propaganda themes, but I suspect that there's enough truth in each of them to persuade many who are uninformed or badly informed around the world. An interesting aspect in all of this is the absence of any ideological justification for apartheid as official policy, thus burying the ghost of Verwoerd, the master architect of apartheid.

Muldergate scandal exposed government propaganda campaign.

"I think one of my favorite headlines was in the Evening Post in Port Elizabeth, "Lies, Lies and More Lies." Isn't that a great headline?'

By Anthony Giffard

Some of South African's propaganda efforts are no different than those used by other countries. For example, South Africa puts out a fairly wide range of publications that are clearly identified as being published by the Department of Information or some other government ministry. These generally are distributed free to whoever is interested in them. They used to have a publication called *South African Digest* that was sort of a summary of news that appeared in South African newspapers. It also included editorials from the Afrikaans press in translation. That was replaced recently by a publication called *Focus on South Africa.*

I still get the stuff. I guess having once been a South African citizen, they have my address. But it's essentially a reprint of articles from the South African newspapers, mostly establishment newspapers — the *Cape Times, The Star,* and so on. But occasionally you'll find pieces in here from *The Sowetan*, for example, *City Press* and a couple of the other somewhat less mainline newspapers. Another one is a rather expensive and glossy publication called *South African Panorama*. It is primarily pictorial. This particular one [holding up magazine] happens to have a lead article on the South African police and the pictures are not of police beating the heads of blacks with truncheons, but instead of policemen taking part in parades and training and going to school and doing all sorts of public spirited things.

C. Anthony Giffard is a professor of communications at the University of Washington in Seattle. He is co-author with William Hachten of *The Press Under Apartheid: Censorship and Repression in South Africa.* Born in South Africa, he worked as a reporter and sub-editor at the *Friend* newspapers in South Africa and at the South African Broadcasting Corporation. He was also director of the Department of Journalism at Rhodes University in Grahamstown, South Africa.

There is a picture here of a policeman with his dog, which describes it as being used in the detection of crime. In addition to these regular publications, they put out occasional sheets. These are put out by the South Africa Foundation, which is a front organization for the South African Information Department. And these are position papers. They come out at somewhat irregular intervals and frequently quote foreigners who are guests of the South African Foundation, and point out that South Africa is not as bad as most people would seem to think.

When things really get bad, they put out extra publications. One such publication is called *South Africa, Mainstay of Southern Africa,* and it came out during the height of the emergency. There's a full-color picture of P.W. Botha on the front. And it tells us, among other things, that South Africa is positively committed and actively involved in contributing to the peace, stability and development of the Southern African region and gives all sorts of arguments to support this point of view. Most countries do this kind of thing. Identical publications are coming out of Germany, France, and most of western Europe, and we can't argue with that kind of publicity. The United States and Canada do this sort thing as well.

In addition to these publications, the government tries to influence people by sponsoring trips, or you might call them junkets, to South Africa by journalists, congressmen, and legislators of various kinds. Normally these are not organized directly by the government. Instead they might be organized by some non-government organization that wants to sponsor a conference perhaps, and government funds are provided to bring people out. Again this is a very common operation.

In addition to the more traditional, what you might call legitimate propaganda, South Africa in the 1970s was engaged in a secret propaganda war which came to be know as Muldergate after Connie Mulder, who was the Minister of Information, and of course the analogy was with Watergate and Nixon.

Muldergate was exposed by the English-language newspapers and by the independent judiciary. There was a commission of inquiry, which I will say more about in a moment. These revelations revealed that South Africa had been engaged in a very widespread, literally worldwide operation, to buy influence through secret means. I think we need to look at the background of this to understand why they felt it necessary to undertake something like that. From the time the

Nationalists came to power in 1948, there's been a belief that South Africa is the victim of an organized press campaign, a campaign that is determined to undermine white rule.

Soon after it came to power, the Nationalist government appointed a press commission, in about 1952. The purpose of this commission was to investigate reporting in South Africa, and particularly reporting that took place in the world's press. The commission sifted through years and years of documents. About 10 years later the first report came out. The second one was about 12 years later. They did extensive content analyses of the major news agencies and concluded, after this laborious effort, that just about everything that came out was negative, biased, distorted, etc. The categories they used, I think, were "very bad", "bad" and "sort of marginally acceptable". Nothing was good or positive in any sense.

There was particular suspicion of foreign correspondents, who, they said, sent out irresponsible or even slanderous reports. And as far as local journalists were concerned, they were concerned about unpatriotic or even treasonous local journalists who acted as stringers for the foreign media.

It's interesting to look at these arguments in the early press council reports and debates in parliament in South Africa in the 1960s, because they really are precursors of the kind of arguments that have been raised by Third World countries in the 1970s, under the rubric of the New International Information Order. Precisely the same kinds of arguments are made — only the negative news events are depicted, whereas positive things, things that take place over a long period of time, are simply ignored by the world's media.

The position certainly became more acute in South Africa in the 1960s. For one thing, when South Africa voted to become a republic in 1961, it was forced to leave the Commonwealth. That followed a whole slew of African nations becoming independent to the north. I can remember, as a young reporter, covering Harold Macmillan's speech to the South African parliament in about 1960 or 1961. He spoke about "the winds of change sweeping South Africa". His statement didn't go over too well with the Nationalist members of parliament at the time.

The fact that these nations were becoming independent meant that South Africa no longer had a buffer to the north. Radio Tanzania, for example, started making frequencies available to the African National Congress and the Pan-Africanist Congress to broadcast shortwave propaganda into South Africa. In addition, South Africa was effectively being isolated in world organizations. They were not only kicked out of the Commonwealth, but isolated in the United Nations and in UNESCO. There were boycotts of South African goods, particularly in Europe, starting with the Nordic countries, and of South African's sports teams.

South Africa was very devoted to sport. No longer could they compete in international rugby matches, or cricket matches. It seemed to hurt more than almost anything else. They were kicked out of all sorts of international organizations. As a result, in 1961, the government decided to set up a Department of Information. The chief moving force was Connie Mulder, the Minister of Information. John Vorster, then the Prime Minister, was very much involved. So were the Head of State Security, and apparently the Minister of Finance, whose help was needed because they had to channel money through secret accounts in Swiss banks in order to do the kinds of things they hoped to achieve.

They appointed Eschel Rhoodie, who had a PhD in sociology. He had been a journalist in some of the Afrikaans newspapers, and was all gung ho to go out and fight the good cause on behalf of South Africa. The new Department of Information was given several tasks. Bill Hachten has alluded to some of the propaganda themes that have been current on South African radio. At the time, these aims were somewhat simpler. In the early 1960s, there had been a huge flight of capital from South Africa. And not only was capital leaving the country, there was also a great deal of emigration. I left at that time.

And so one of the propaganda themes was to portray the country as a stable, profitable environment for investment and a good place for Europeans to immigrate to. At that time, South Africa did not rely on training the indigenous black population for its trained man power needs, but on bringing in European immigrants. And that had pretty well dried up after Sharpeville.

The second major theme was to stress the importance of South Africa to the West, particularly in terms of strategic minerals, South Africa's role in the two world wars on behalf of the allied forces, and the fact that it was the guardian of the strategic sea routes around the Cape, which carried most of the world's oil traffic, and still do to a large extent. They felt that South Africa should be seen as a bastion of Western civilization at the tip of a rapidly darkening continent, and many South Africans genuinely believed this. They had this idea that they were put there by God in the 17th century in order to bring Christianity and civilization to Africa.

With these themes in mind then, starting in about 1972, they began a propaganda operation in earnest. Connie Mulder appointed Rhoodie as a Secretary for Information. And it seems that one of the first projects they undertook was a *Time*-style news magazine called *To The Point,* which was intended to counter the perceived left-wing orientation of much of the world's press. It wasn't a bad magazine in some ways. It was one of the few magazines that focused on events in Africa, and nobody else was doing this at the time. But it transpired later that *To The Point* was funded by the South African government. They provided the funds to start it through a front man, a citizen of the Netherlands. And once the magazine was under way, the South African government bought large numbers of copies of this magazine, which they then distributed to people worldwide, free of charge. It went to newspapers and influential people around the world.

It was discovered later, when all of this was revealed, that there was a secret agreement between *To The Point* and the Information Department, that the magazine would never attack apartheid or white rule or any of the other tenets of the Nationalist government. Within South Africa, there was a rather difficult approach taken.

There are four major press groups in South Africa, two of them English, two of them Afrikaans, and all are quite apart from the alternative media that we've been hearing about recently. And of those press groups, by far the most critical of the government, was a string of newspapers, a chain of newspapers then called SAAN, or South African Association of Newspapers, with the Rand Daily Mail as its flagship, but also with some very other outspoken newspapers, including the *Cape Times* in Cape Town, the *Eastern Province Herald,* and so on, five or six other newspapers around the country. The biggest chain was the Argus group, including Harvey Tyson's *Star,* but SAAN was by far the most aggressive in countering government policies. But SAAN wasn't making much money. In fact, because of the political line they were taking, they were not very popular with white readers and as a result, not many advertisers were buying space in its papers, and the company was losing money.

It seemed ripe for a takeover. And the approach came from a rather unexpected source, a fertilizer salesman called Louis Luyt, who had built up a fertilizer empire in South Africa. He announced that he was going to buy control of SAAN and offered twice the current share value to take over this entire group. There was a lot of consternation in English circles at the time, as you can imagine. And when his offer was spurned, he doubled the amount that he was offering, now about four or fives times the going rate for the shares. You know, he was doing this as a patriotic act, to improve the kind of coverage of South Africa. And eventually a group of South African businessmen got together and formed a trust and bought 20 per cent of the SAAN shares, and since the Argus company held 30 per cent of the shares, it meant that the company was safe from the takeover from the likes of Louis Luyt.

Spurred by SAAN, Luyt announced that he was going to start his own English-language newspaper. The paper would be called *The Citizen*. This was announced in early 1976, I think it must have been. You must understand why Luyt decided to start an English-language newspaper in a market that already was overcrowded. Johannesburg, at that time a city of roughly a million white people, plus at least another million blacks, was already being served by something like five different newspapers. There were two English-language newspapers, one morning, one afternoon; two Afrikaans-language newspapers, one morning and one afternoon; plus a newspaper *The World,* that was serving the black community.

Most cities the size of Johannesburg in the United States or Canada would have two newspapers, or only one. But here Luyt was coming in and saying that he was going start a new newspaper to compete head-on with the *Rand Daily Mail* in the Johannesburg morning field, which sounded like a kind of suicidal approach. Nevertheless, *The Citizen* got off the ground in September of 1976. It was a tabloid. It proved to be strongly pro-government in its views. It provided the government viewpoint for conservative English-speaking South Africans.

And perhaps more important from the government's point of view, it made available in English, for the first time, pro-government views that could be picked up by foreign correspondents. Very few foreign correspondents can read or understand Afrikaans. And since the English-language newspapers were uniformly hostile to the government, and the Afrikaans newspapers — which supported government policy — couldn't be read by the foreign correspondents, the feeling was that if they were exposed to these things in their own language, they might be more inclined to pick up news from the English-language press, in this case supporting government policy.

The Citizen quickly cut into the *Rand Daily Mail's* white readership. *The Mail* was in a somewhat precarious position to begin with. And *The Citizen* drew off many of its more conservative white readers in the morning area. As a result, *The Mail* quickly had a preponderance of black readers. In fact, at the time The Mail folded, it had something like 72 per cent black readership. Now that sounds like a perfectly acceptable thing, except that most of the advertisers weren't interested in reaching black readers whom they felt couldn't afford to buy the products that they wanted to advertise. And so *The Citizen* was drawing off advertising and The Mail was getting increasingly isolated in that respect.

The Citizen took a very strong pro-government line. To give one example, when Steve Biko died in a police van on his way from the coast up to Johannesburg, *The Citizen* initially supported the government line that he had died of natural causes. When an inquest proved that he died of massive head injuries, *The Citizen* suggested he had committed suicide by banging his head against the wall. *The Mail* didn't take this challenge lying down. They obviously smelled a rat. And reporters for *The Mail* and its companion newspapers, *The Sunday Times* and *The Sunday Express*, began to track rumors of Department of Information involvement in *The Citizen* and in various other activities.

They were quickly jumped on by the government. When two South African newspapers even suggested that *To The Point* was being funded by government, they were dragged in front of the Press Council, sort of a watchdog committee, and Rhoodie swore under oath that *To The Point* was not being sponsored by the government. Mulder, who knew that it was, and Vorster, who also knew, said nothing to contradict this. Both newspapers were fined large amounts and ordered to print an apology and a retraction. But the newspapers couldn't really get to the root of this, partly because of the *Official Secrets Act,* and partly because of government determination to cover up what was going on.

The real lead to the story came from a somewhat unexpected source, in that the government had appointed a one-man commission of inquiry under Judge Anton Mostert, who was investigating violations of Exchange Control Regulations. South Africa had very strict exchange control regulations in place as a result of the exodus of capital. You couldn't take much money out of the country with you even if you emigrated. And there were all sorts of rumors that these were being circumvented. Mostert was looking into what was going on, and discovered that large sums of money had been loaned through Swiss banks in order to support secret projects by the Information Department, including *To The Point* and *The Citizen*.

Mulder announced that he was going to release this information, and Vorster tried to block it. The courts ruled that he could go ahead and do so anyway. And the next morning there were huge headlines in the South African newspapers. I've never seen headlines quite that large in papers. They were about a 72-point, which is one inch high. These findings were trumpeted not only in the English newspapers but in the Afrikaans newspapers, because there was a fight going on between different factions of the Nationalist party at the time, one of which supported Mulder and the other supported Vorster. As a result, even the Afrikaans newspapers got involved in this.

The one conspicuous exception, by the way, was the South African Broadcasting Corporation, which did not mention a word of Mostert's findings on its newscast that night. And so people who wanted to know what was going on would not have been listening to the radio. They would have had to read the newspaper to find out what was happening. That is very typical of other kinds of coverage as well.

The upshot of all this is that eventually Mulder, who was the sort of heir apparent to Vorster was forced to resign. *The Rand Daily Mail*'s joyful headline on this [holding up newspaper] was, "Mulder Quits". The Information Department had spent something like $64 million, which doesn't sound like a lot in Canadian terms these days, but certainly was a great deal in South Africa at the time.

I think one of my favorite headlines was in the *Evening Post* in Port Elizabeth, [holding up newspaper], "Lies, Lies and More Lies." Isn't that a great headline? The way they spread that over the page, fantastic coverage! Most of these revelations dealt with what was going on in South Africa. But as a result of the pressures, the government was forced to appoint a commission of inquiry. And this revealed that South Africa had also undertaken a large number of secret projects abroad to try and influence public opinion in favor of the South African position.

And so, there was a series of advertisements run in newspapers abroad, ostensibly coming from a group called the Club of Ten. They bought full-page advertisements in newspapers like *The Times, The Guardian, The Telegraph, The Washington Post, The New York Times, The Montreal Star* and a couple of other publications in

Canada. And the theme of these ads was that South Africa was being unfairly criticized by groups like the World Council of Churches and the United Nations.

They were very aggressive. They pointed out the double standards and the hypocrisy of the criticism focused on South Africa. Supposedly, the Club of Ten consisted of 10 South African businessmen, rich businessmen who were concerned about the country's image abroad. In fact, there was only one visible person, a London lawyer called Gerald Sparrow, who it later turned out was the sole member of the Club of Ten, and was getting all his money from the Information Department.

There is a publisher in the American Midwest, specifically in Illinois and Michigan, called John McGoff, who owned a string of daily and weekly newspapers and was known for his conservative views. It turned out, through this investigation, that McGoff had been given something like $10 million by the South African government in order to buy the failing *Washington Star*. *The Washington Post* was very successful, but *The Washington Star* was losing money. They were looking for a buyer, and McGoff put in a bid for *The Washington Star*. They didn't accept his bid. It was sold to a Texan instead, for even more money.

Instead, McGoff bought *The Sacramento Union* in California, using this money. He also bought a 50 per cent share in UPI Television News, which is the world's second-largest producer and distributor of TV news film. The intention apparently was to use this as a vehicle for distributing South African television film, giving a much more positive image of the country. When the scandal broke, McGoff was forced to sell the paper. He returned about $5 million of the money to South Africa and the other $5 million, plus the interest, was simply written off by the South African government. There were various attempts to prosecute McGoff for acting as a foreign agent without registering with the government. Recently, the statute of limitations expired and so he was let off the hook.

Money was channeled into congressional senate races in the United States to help defeat South Africa's enemies. They had all sorts of front organizations for journalists and other opinion-makers — things like the Foreign Affairs Association, The Institute For the Study of Plural Societies, and so on, which were organizing trips and conferences in South Africa. In Europe, Information Department funds were used to buy publishing houses. They tried to buy *The Observer*, *The Telegraph* and a couple of other newspapers. Most of this seems to have come to an end with the disclosures in the late 1970s. But the government made it clear at the time that there were still certain projects that would be continued, and of course they didn't tell anybody what those projects were.

There are some rather suspicious suggestions or clues. Ameen Akhalwaya was telling me that he is forced to keep his ad rates artificially low for his newspaper, because the government is subsidizing a pro-apartheid journal in competition with his own. Harvey Tyson says that *The Citizen,* although it has fewer advertisements then *The Star,* prints more pages. And the suggestion is, there must be some kind of money coming from the outside. The only link, or the only suggestion, that I have been able to trace for continued external operations is that when *The Washington Star* folded, it was replaced by *The Washington Times. The Washington Times* is funded by the Unification Church. It's a very conservative newspaper and tends to be quite supportive of the South African position, and of the Republican position, vis-à-vis South Africa.

When *The Washington Times* was started, McGoff became a member of the board, and McGoff's editor-in-chief, a man called James Whelan, became the first editor of *The Washington Times.* I'm not suggesting there is any connection between these things, but at least it provides us with some food for thought.

ANC image distorted by government propaganda

"When you support us, you are not supporting some distant people, some naked Africans in the jungles of Africa. You are promoting your own cause, which is the fight against racism wherever it rears its ugly head."

By Francis Meli

I am not long-winded. But my short contribution, like a mini-skirt, will cover everything. The African National Congress wishes to put on record its appreciation for being invited to this conference.

I'll try and give you a picture of the problems that the African National Congress is faced with in the field of propaganda externally. Apartheid propaganda internationally reflects the aggressive policies of the regime. It is said that apartheid means separation of races. But in fact, apartheid means more than that. It also means inequality. The theories of apartheid tell us biological differences lead to conflicts. But if we're to believe that, we'd find it difficult to explain the many marriages in this world.

In the 1984-86 upheavals, foreign correspondents, especially cameramen, were very busy covering these events. The problem was that they were never seen on the side of the people. They stood behind the South African Defence Force police. What you saw on television were people killed, running away, fleeing. Seldom did you see people advancing. The result was that the international community responded to these events in a curious way. They started to pity us, and pity is not the same thing as solidarity. These images and stereotypes, created by cameramen, tended to distort our reality and our struggle.

Francis Meli was born in Cambridge Location in the southeastern part of South Africa. An orphan, he grew up under the apartheid system. When he started school, Meli became involved with the African National Congress (ANC) and the African Students Association (ASA). He left his homeland to study abroad. In 1973 he earned a PhD in history in the German Democratic Republic. He was elected to the National Executive Committee of the ANC in 1985. Since 1977, he has served as editor of *Sechaba,* the official organ of the ANC.

The real source of this stereotype is the apartheid regime. Through television, radio and pamphlets, the ANC is portrayed as terrorists or hijackers or reckless communists. A pamphlet called *Talking With the ANC* went so far as to maintain that of the 30 members of the National Executive Committee in 1985, 23 were either members or active supporters of the South African Communist Party. The ANC is therefore portrayed as a communist-front organization. This brings me to a related question. What is the relevance of our struggle to the Canadians?

The mere existence of apartheid is an encouragement, is an inspiration, to racists all over the world. And that includes Canada. In other words, when you support us, you are not supporting some distant people, some naked Africans in the jungles of Africa. You are promoting your own cause, which is the fight against racism wherever it rears its ugly head. What do we mean when we say your struggle is our struggle? What is the relationship between the ANC and world peace? Canadians are very much involved in the question of world peace. The ANC is very much involved in the armed struggle. How can a blood-thirsty man like me talk about world peace — a man who is involved in the armed struggle?

It is usually said that apartheid is a threat to world peace. It might be true, but look at it from the point of view of Namibians, Angolans and South Africa's blacks. Apartheid is more than a threat to world peace. Apartheid is a killer. It is a violation of peace. We see a connection between our struggle against apartheid and a struggle for world peace. In fighting for our liberation, we are actually fighting for world peace. South Africa says it must protect shipping in the Indian Ocean against Soviet penetration. That means the Indian Ocean must be militarized — not only the Indian Ocean, but also all the islands around there, because of the threat of Soviet penetration.

Actually, what Soviet penetration means is that oil from the Middle East comes to western Europe and comes to this part of the world via South Africa, and therefore the Indian Ocean shipping lanes have to be militarized, so that this oil from the Middle East can reach this part of the world safely. In other words, you have a role to play in the demilitarization of the Indian Ocean.

I just want to say a word about racism, because this is one problem we're facing in South Africa. There are some people who would believe that once you destroy apartheid, everything will be fine in South Africa. Such arguments ignore the simple fact that racism has a dynamism of its own, has its own momentum. Racism has economic roots besides a political purpose. Racism can have a momentum of its own among common people — people who have no economic interests in the system, people who are suffering themselves, but they can become racists. It is therefore very important to teach the international community about the dangers of racism. In South Africa we're not just fighting against apartheid. Our anti-racist struggle has an anti-colonial dimension, and is basically anti-imperialist.

Back to the foreign journalists. While the detainees were on a hunger strike in South Africa, some world newspapers were more concerned with Olivia Forsythe, who is supposed to have infiltrated the ANC and returned to South Africa from Angola, where she was held by the British. The truth is that in Angola, Olivia Forsythe was in detention, and this is not the place where you can get vital information about the ANC. She was in a jail. All I'm saying is that journalists looking for juicy and sensational stories bypass us and look for information about us somewhere else, forgetting that we, the ANC, are also a source of information.

My contribution would be incomplete if I did not discuss the question of sanctions and the independence of Namibia. Some people say sanctions don't work. Others say that sanctions will hurt blacks most. But sanctions did contribute to the defeat of the South African Defense Force in southern Angola. It is true that the courage and military skills of the Cubans, Angolans, and Namibians were the decisive force. But the racists lost their superiority. Their aging Mirages were no match for the more sophisticated weapons used by the Cubans and Angolans, thanks to sanctions. That means, if we push the Canadian government to a point where it can apply sanctions, you will be contributing to our struggle.

The ANC has never for a moment believed that sanctions will bring the Pretoria regime to its knees. Sanctions are not the opposite of armed struggle. What we are saying is that sanctions will weaken the apartheid economy. They will shorten the lifespan of apartheid and therefore lessen the flow of blood in the streets of South Africa. This will be your contribution to that struggle.

The ANC is very much involved in the campaign against Pretoria's disinformation and deception techniques. It publishes a number of journals, including *Sechaba*, its official organ.

Radio Freedom broadcasts from Luanda, Lusaka and elsewhere. The advantage of *Radio Freedom* is that you don't have to be literate to understand it. It broadcasts also in African languages concerning acceptance of the ANC.

One of the lies propagated in western Europe and America, and this includes Canada, is that Botha is a reformist who cannot implement his reforms because of the fear of a right-wing backlash, and because of the inflexibility of the ANC and the mass democratic movement. The problem is that the right wing is there because of apartheid. Remove apartheid from South Africa, and then there is no right wing.

Secondly, reforms in South Africa are not the opposite of repression. Reforms and repression are two sides of the same coin. How do we, all of us, including the international community, defeat apartheid? Can we defeat apartheid? All of us must understand our enemy, his allies, and his strengths and weaknesses. I cannot dwell on this point except to say our struggle is for national liberation of the blacks, especially the Africans. These people have been disadvantaged, colonized for more than 300 years — colonized not in Europe but in Pretoria. That is why we call it "colonialization of a special type".

We are fighting for the seizure of power, and not reforms. We use all methods towards this goal — strikes, demonstrations, school boycotts, etc. We involve everybody, the workers, youths, women, religious people and the rural masses. The democratically minded whites must be involved in this struggle, because they cannot be free as long as the black man is not free in South Africa. The ANC has a special role in this struggle, not because it demands that, but because the ANC is the only organization in South Africa which is engaged in armed struggle. At times, we have to pay dearly for that.

Recently, two whites died at Alice Park and the international community demanded that the ANC must apologize for two whites. They asked, "Are you becoming terrorists now? Have you changed your strategies to soft targets?" The ANC never said that it was responsible for that operation, but because we are known to be the only operation engaged in armed struggle in South Africa, we have to pay dearly. Talking about armed struggle in South Africa, I think this is one of the greatest challenges that will face the international community in the coming years. This is partly due to this kith and kin business. To explain that, let me give you an anecdote.

It is said a white liberal in South Africa is like a boy who stands on a cliff and sees a big dog chasing a half-naked African. He is half-naked because there is no money to buy clothes. The white liberal screams, "Oh, God, that dog is going to tear that man to pieces." The African turns and stabs the dog to death with his big knife. The liberal screams, "Oh, what a beautiful dog that was!" I hope you're not all white liberals.

Canadians shouldn't be smug about South Africa.

"The poor housing, health and situation of Canada's Indians is as good an indication of a racist society as an openly avowed policy of racial supremacy."

By Angus Gunn

I want to deal as succinctly as I can with two things. First: preparing people to identify and cope with propaganda, with parallel recognition of the limitations of benefits of the mass media in that process. Second: looking ahead to the worldwide technological revolution as a powerful and comprehensive answer to censorship.

I'm a teacher and my job is to make people think, especially to think critically and skeptically about the data that was fed to them in today's information explosion, so they are not fooled by propaganda, whether it comes from the South African government or any other source. In Canada, we are living in a society of incredible freedom compared with the rest of the world. It never enters our heads that a dictatorial regime could smother us in a very short time. The notion that eternal vigilance is the price of liberty is, to most of us, a cute phrase for English essays.

Let me say in a couple of sentences what this means in terms of coping with South African propaganda. We will never be able to distinguish South African fact from propaganda unless we have a basic framework of knowledge about that country that enables us to put news or pictures or words into a context that is familiar to us. We won't get that framework from the media, either print or video. They can't do it even with the series of documentaries.

Angus Gunn is the author of a new book, *South Africa: A World Challenged.* Professor emeritus of social and educational studies at the University of British Columbia, he has twice been a visiting scholar at Rhodes University in Grahamstown, South Africa. His published views have been generally sympathetic to the South African government. He was president of a private educational foundation which seeks to assist South African blacks. He was assistant director of educational research with the U.S. National Science Foundation. He lives in West Vancouver, B.C.

The media of press and television are indispensable for what they do, keeping us in touch with world developments and world events as they occur. But when it comes to a meaningful context or identifying facts and distinguishing propaganda, we have to learn it.

Learning is a thing that learners do, and it's not to be confused with listening to lectures or watching the tube or even reading books, good as all of these things are. To acquire an understanding of the South African context, so that it becomes familiar to us, involves much more than detailed information. It requires dealing with our prejudices, sorting out our existing knowledge and looking squarely at our motives and interests. If I go to some of the black private in-service centres in the black communities of South Africa as I hope to do this summer, and if I try to teach them some history, say European history, I would not do it in the way that I would do it here. I would first begin with teaching something about their own cultural history and establish, within that framework, a conceptual framework of understanding before I began to introduce another history.

Westerners need to make many adjustments when looking at South Africa. Europeans continue to see it as delayed colonial territory to be resolved like all the others of Africa. The United States sees it as a delayed civil rights struggle. And in Canada, we have our own myopia. A racist society is known by its works. The poor housing, health and situation of Canada's Indians is as good an indication of a racist society as an openly avowed policy of racial supremacy.

Now whatever be the truth and observation of these things, they are not adequate to cope with an understanding of the reality of South Africa. Unless we understand backgrounds, our own backgrounds, and distinguish them from the real South African situations, we will end up with caricatures and we will be easy prey for whatever lobby or propaganda next comes our way.

It is not an easy task that I am talking about. It's an essential task, and one that we must undertake if we are going to influence public policy and media content in the right directions and avoid being mislead. We need to recognize at the same time the limitations of the mass media, while they are enormously valuable to us in the way in which I indicated. Every journalist knows that stories about power, crime, sex, money, tragedy and racism are the things that sell newspapers and interest television watchers. Selling papers or increasing viewing audiences is of course first priority for publisher and broadcaster alike.

By definition, news deals with the extraordinary. Hence, ordinary events or average conditions appear less frequently in the mass media. As a result, we are given a skewed image of the world, a record of occasional, often bizarre events, that will pique our interest long enough for the advertiser to make his pitch. These distorted pictures of life are harmless when they come from local or familiar places. Experiences and other sorts of information provide a balance. It's a very different story when the report comes from lesser-known regions. Caricatures of people and countries become standard fare.

In an earlier generation, when print was the principal medium, libraries provided balance, offsetting the limitations of the newspaper. It is much more difficult to compensate for television bias. For most people, seeing is believing. There is no felt need for additional information. The fact that a 30-second clip is only a partial image of the event, that audience interest dominates item selection, and that the personal philosophy of a network anchor person, or his mentors, also affect choices, are largely lost on the viewer. The immediacy, color, action and fascination of the story carry their own intrinsic authenticity.

Well, there's the problem. And maybe we can ask, why is there so little political attempt in the schools, in the universities of Canada, to develop an adequate context on this extremely important part of the world, in the minds of the young? Canada, because of its Commonwealth associations and because of its very high profile role in that organization, especially now that the Commonwealth University of Learning has been established in my own city of Vancouver, is well-placed to give leadership here. South Africa is surrounded by half a dozen Commonwealth countries, and perhaps and hopefully, Namibia will be a seventh. So we ought to be doing something about this context in our schools and our universities. I have difficulty at the moment thinking of a single institution that does this in any level of depth, and in the kind of depth that is needed.

One big part of the context, just to round out that part of my presentation, is that we need to get a real sense of South African history. Why did these men behave in such a vicious way? Aren't they part of the so-called homo sapiens just like the rest of us? We wouldn't do that sort of thing, would we? I don't know the answer to that, because I think that a person's history has much to do with his or her behavior. Think of these items. Within living memory, those very people who are now in government were so poor — I'm talking about the early years of this century — that their black neighbors would have bought them out if Lord Milner, the British governor, had not interfered. I wonder if this is why Allan Payton talks about their feelings of fear and hatred towards blacks. They hardly thought about blacks in the 150 years, from 1800 to 1950, because they were obsessed with deep resentment toward the English.

And as a man born in Scotland, I empathize with that dislike. When the mother of the present Queen visited South Africa in the '30s, she was inspecting a guard of honor, and an Afrikaner jumped out of the line and said, "I hate the English!" And the Queen, without missing a beat, turned around and said, "I quite understand. I'm Scottish." Is this the reason why they are so hateful and resentful towards English-speaking countries? Only within the past 10 years have present government members become really acquainted with television. Couple that with the fact that most of them are speaking in a second language when they're interviewed by Western journalists. It's like me trying to use my five years of French and dealing with the nuances of a very complex subject. Couple these two things together, you have this sort of clumsy performance that we're familiar with.

A classic was the debacle that we saw on *Nightline* with Ted Koppel interviewing Pik Botha a short time ago. So to return to the central theme of fighting propaganda, some have suggested that South Africa be totally isolated from the Western world as a counteraction, while still maintaining the pressure for change. I think this is a short-sighted view, and I like Sharon Sopher's courageous outlook. There are many reasons why we should persist. We heard many of them here already, this week. And there are also the lesser-known environmental concerns that fortunately humanity is beginning to look at for the first time in a serious way.

Our global village is fast becoming a more intimate community every year. To isolate a community the size of South Africa carries risks for the rest of Africa and for the whole world. You take the Kalahari and Sahara deserts, for example. They are merging at the rate of a 160 kilometres a year, because the settlement practice is an agricultural practice. Some common agreements are needed. The ozone layer over Antarctica will receive more damage with consequent cancer risks for the whole world unless South Africa joins Europe and North America in banning the chemicals that affect it.

So, in summary, in my first point, I would like to say this. Developing an adequate background knowledge that will enable us to spot propaganda and expose it is better than just blandly condemning the source.

Secondly, and briefly, I want to touch on the technological revolution, with particular reference to censorship. We deplore the loss of television coverage in the townships. This may not be the cataclysmic event and loss that is seems to be at first glance. While film continues to see a bright future, the fate of the big mass media television networks is less certain. Costs are skyrocketing and credibility is waning. What about nuclear power? Wouldn't it be better for all of South Africa's nuclear installations if they were under the aegis of the International Atomic Energy Agency?

In North America, in the last decade and a half, acceptance of the reliability of television information dropped from 30 per cent to 25 per cent of viewers. Newspapers have gone from 25 to 20, and for some extraordinary reason, confidence in statements from the military has risen in the same period. Part of the reason for the drop relates to the power and prestige that have come to be identified with these mass media. People react negatively to this sort of thing, just as they do towards big business or big unions or big government. I think there is another reason too. The shift, as Patrick Nagle described it for us, from the clinical separation between personal opinion and the facts of a story, to the journalist's high involvement in personal reporting, has created uncertainty as to what is story, what is fact, and what is opinion.

Whatever the reason, the fate of the mass media networks, as we have known them, is most likely to be affected negatively by advances in technology. We are all familiar with the inroads of the video and the VCR on television, and likewise, the impact of the computer on the newspaper. In fact, the newest generation of computers can reproduce and instantly update color pictures by video disks. So that given the volume that will bring the cost under control, the video and the VCR can be replaced. There is a further development, one that will profoundly affect censorship. Indeed, the awareness of this particular development has already filtered through to dictatorships worldwide, rendering obsolete every possible attempt of theirs to control the inflow of information to their territories.

I've wondered if this development is the reason behind the general thaw in world relations over the last three years. I refer to satellite communications, coupled with the newer minute antennas that can be folded and placed inside a paperback, so that it is impossible for authoritarian governments to prevent their reception to people within their country. You don't need electricity for reception. You can work from batteries and on solar power or you can do what they do in the Third World areas of India. You have the boys pedaling their bicycles to generate the power, while everybody else can watch the television.

And there is a satellite within reach of Southern Africa at the present time that could beam 100 channels into black townships. If you're worried about land lines being cut, you can use the same satellite in telephone links to send pictures to these townships. I don't have any information on outflow capability, but it cannot be far behind. What I'm saying here in essence is, the technological revolution is going to make censorship look ridiculous, and in fact it will kill it fully, given the short time and given the persistence on our part in the present situation.

I am very optimistic about the future of South Africa if we and others like us are willing to do our homework and stick with the opportunities we have. Persistence and stickability are not North American virtues, but we can acquire them by observing our South African black brothers and sisters.

Let me conclude with one statement. We can learn to identify and deal with propaganda, while hanging in with those who are working for a better future South Africa, knowing that the emerging technological revolution will soon blow the lid off of every vestige of censorship.

Resolutions adopted
by the conference

That this conference, "South Africa: Getting the Real Story", organized by the University of Regina School of Journalism and Communications, Regina, Saskatchewan, March 16-18, 1989, having discussed the media in South Africa, and the flow of information between South Africa and the rest of the world, proposes the following:

1. To assist the alternative media in South Africa, and those sections of the establishment media involved in the struggle against apartheid, in identifying resources and technical assistance.

   Similar assistance must also be provided for the national liberation movements and those progressive South Africans living outside the country who are involved in media and public information.

   Universities and schools of journalism can provide training in such areas as research, writing and other aspects of the profession. Newspapers, news agencies, radio and TV stations can provide practical training.

2. To work closely with the national liberation movement, the alternative media, the anti-apartheid establishment media, and the democratic movement in South Africa, to publicize the struggle for freedom, justice and human rights in South Africa.

3. To strengthen the media in the African frontline states to enable them to resist South Africa's propaganda campaigns, and to support the national liberation movements and the alternative media in providing training and technical assistance. Such assistance must include financial assistance to strengthen existing institutions in the African frontline states.

4. To campaign for protection for journalists and other media workers in South Africa.

162 Getting the Real Story

5. To analyze and closely monitor the system of censorship in South Africa.

6. To work closely with Article 19 and other international institutions in South Africa which publicize censorship in South Africa.

7. To communicate to the international media the contents of this proposal and the proceedings of this conference, so as to make them aware of the frustrations of black South African journalists who feel that the international media remain largely insensitive to their plight.

8. To promote greater co-operation among the established media and alternative media in Canada and other countries to support freedom of press and the struggle for justice in South Africa, and in heightening public awareness in Canada and other countries about the situation in South Africa and the frontline states.

9. To urge the Canadian media to report regularly on South Africa's destabilization in the frontline states and the effects that such destabilization have on the economic, social and cultural realities in Southern Africa. The particular plight of Mozambique requires closer attention.

10. To monitor and expose the South African government's program of disinformation and press manipulation in Canada.

11. To commend the Canadian government for the assistance it provides to South African media attacked by the South African regime, particular the independent media.

The conference urges the Canadian government to expend this assistance, but this assistance must not be extended at the expense of other measures called for by the democratic movement in South Africa.

The conference is singing External's song.

Michael Valpy *was* **The Globe and Mail's** *Africa correspondent from 1984 through 1987, during which time he won two National Newspaper Awards for foreign reporting. He now is a* **Globe** *columnist based in Toronto. He was invited to speak at the conference, and initially accepted. But then he decided not to attend, and issued the following statement:*

I am boycotting the conference on South Africa organized by the University of Regina's School of Journalism and Communications. I frankly hope other people will do the same — and send a message to the Canadian government that it is betraying the opponents of apartheid around the world and betraying the honor of the people of Canada here at home.

This conference is largely paid for by the Canadian government and is structured so as to serve as a vehicle for Ottawa's intentions to renege on its once-commendable South African policy.

I was scheduled to take part as chairman of a panel discussion. I cancelled on the day I found out that the conference's focus would be on South African censorship and propaganda and that the Department of External Affairs was looking after most of the bills with a donation of $42,000.

Nothing would be wrong with a conference on South African propaganda and censorship — if it were not that these are the subjects Ottawa wants Canadians to talk about, and that what Ottawa does not want Canadians to talk about is the government's abandoned promise to take the strongest action against South Africa if it did not end apartheid and move toward a democratic multi-racial state.

Stay with me while I take you through the history. In the summer of 1985, Commonwealth leaders — including Canada's Brian Mulroney — agreed at their Nassau summit to impose some voluntary economic sanctions against South Africa.

In the fall of 1985, Prime Minister Mulroney told the United Nations General Assembly that if the South African government did not dismantle apartheid and open a dialogue on full internal democracy, Canada would impose full and mandatory sanctions and possibly sever diplomatic relations.

In February 1987, at the end of his African visit, Mulroney said he was returning to Canada with the "sad conclusion . . . that the way of dialogue (in South Africa) is not making progress, but is regressing." Asked if this meant Canada would turn its voluntary sanctions into mandatory ones, Mulroney became puzzlingly vague, saying only that Canada would act in concert with its allies.

In October 1987, at the Commonwealth summit in Vancouver, Mulroney said in an interview he had seen nothing to indicate South Africa was dismantling apartheid or moving toward a democratic state. Asked if this meant Canada was moving toward severing diplomatic relations, he replied:

> We are coming closer to that, yes. We are moving. The silence and the absence of dialogue takes us closer to that. Canada cannot be (merely) benignly interested in the greatest moral debate that is going on. Canada has to be on the high ground and provide leadership to its friends and allies around the world.

In June 1988, at the summit meeting in Toronto of the world's industrialized nations, the G-7, Mulroney tried to press the case of full and mandatory sanctions with Thatcher's Britain, Reagan's America, Kohl's West Germany, and with that money-banking beneficiary of sanctions-busting, Japan. He got nowhere.

Two months later, in August 1988, Ottawa began its big lie. The occasion was the meeting of the Commonwealth's committee of foreign ministers on southern Africa. External Affairs suddenly announced — with massive amounts of expensive publicity and hired impresarios — that South African censorship and propaganda were now the prime issues, no longer sanctions. To support this message, External Affairs spent hundreds of thousands of dollars to assemble speakers, musicians, artists. In the biggest single piece of hoopla, thousands of Torontonians were assembled to light candles for the cause of South African truth.

Commonwealth Foreign Ministers from Africa caught on quickly. On the day the conference began, the main headline on *The Globe and Mail's* front page read: "Ottawa deflection of sanctions issue angers delegates."

To quote Canada's leading academic expert on South Africa, Professor Linda Freeman of Carleton University:

> (External Affairs Minister) Joe Clark's attempt to focus the delegates' attention on the minor Canadian project of combating South African censorship and propaganda and away from the main issue of wider and tougher sanctions angered and distressed the Commonwealth Secretary-General and the African delegations.
>
> In exasperation, one African foreign minister asked Clark in a closed session what his problem was. Clark suggested that the Canadian public did not want a stronger policy — (although) as the African minister pointed out, polls show that half of all Canadians would support tougher measures.

Since the Prime Minister's honorable speech to the UN General Assembly in 1985, the South African government has travelled an undeviating path of greater political repression. Since 1985, elements of petty apartheid — whites-only toilets, whites-only recreation facilities — have been re-instated. Since 1985, more and more voices of opposition have been silenced. Since 1985, not one step has been taken toward the dismantling of racism and the creation of a democratic state.

Since 1985, Canada's trade with South Africa has increased. Since 1985, the government of Brian Mulroney has taken no steps to make Canada's economic sanctions either full or mandatory. Canada's two-way trade with South African is still about $200 million annually. The Canadian government has not kept its pledge to discourage scientific co-operation. South Africans were permitted to attend three officially sponsored conferences in Canada. Canadian companies such as Canadian Pacific have been involved in sanction busting.

What has happened is that Canada's honorable South Africa policy has never been more than Brian Mulroney's South Africa policy.

Mulroney has never had the support of Cabinet — some of whose members, such as John Crosbie, have visited South Africa at Pretoria's invitation. A majority of Cabinet is philosophically opposed to tampering with business, whatever the cause. Others still hold to the belief that Pretoria's racist government is the bulwark against communism in southern Africa.

Mulroney also has never had the support of External Affairs, perhaps the most spineless of Canadian ministries. External's basic creed is to dislike any policy that puts Canada at odds with the foreign policies of the United States and, to a lesser degree, Britain.

Thus, as Stephen Lewis, Canada's former ambassador to the UN, has put it with regard to South Africa, "Canada is on the verge of dereliction to our commitment."

In the meantime, External Affairs makes money available for a conference such as this one, to talk about censorship and propaganda. Well, whose propaganda?

Sat Kumar, director of the School of Journalism, says that although External Affairs has paid for the conference and suggested speakers, it has had no control over "editorial content". My reply is that External Affairs does not need control; the conference is singing External's song.

The issue we are trying to confront is censorship — the basic right of a citizen to express himself.

*At the close of his presentation to the conference, Southam News Africa bureau chief Patrick Nagle made the following statement. It was in reference to the fact that Michael Valpy, former African correspondent for **The Globe and Mail**, had originally agreed to speak at the conference, but subsequently withdrew. Mr. Valpy made public comments about his decision to withdraw, and appeared on CBC television with Joe Thloloe, deputy-editor of **The Sowetan**, who was a speaker at the conference:*

Michael Valpy from Toronto has boycotted this conference, he says, "as a matter of principle." He believes the conference should not be about censorship because this permits the Canadian government to manipulate the agenda to their advantage and away from the issue of sanctions, which the Canadian government wants to avoid.

In short, Michael has imposed a sanction on us. I regard this as an unhappy self-serving position that should not deflect the aim of this conference. The sanctions debate in Canada is a domestic, political issue demanding that these courageous people, my colleagues in South Africa, take sides on Brian Mulroney's problems with John Turner and Ed Broadbent. That is both perverse and irrational.

Valpy knows from personal experience that it is against the law of South Africa for a South African citizen to promote development of sanctions either inside or outside their country. The issue we are trying to confront is censorship — the basic right of a citizen to express himself. The Salman Rushdie situation has attracted world attention because of the theatrical aspect of the threat to Rushdie's life. The South African situation is far more banal. Hundreds of journalists and authors live and work daily under a threat of retribution that is not as violent as that of the Ayatollah, but the South African threat comes from exactly the same intellectual source — the zealous enforcement of an ideal that is totally at odds with modern civilized society.

That is the principle that brought me here to this conference, and if Valpy wants to boycott that principle, well and good. I mean, it is a free country.

But I would like to apologize personally to Joe Thloloe for the appalling lack of professionalism displayed by some of my Canadian colleagues. Joe was naturally unaware of this trivial controversy when he agreed to appear on a Canadian Broadcasting Corporation interview show. He handled himself very graciously, despite not being advised of the substance of this issue. In Canadian journalism, this is called blind-siding, and it is an entirely inappropriate tactic to use on such a distinguished guest to our country.